EMPOWERMENT
—— through ——
LEARNING

'*Empowerment Through Learning* is a timely and thoughtful contribution to the world of education. It serves as a powerful reminder that every experience—whether a triumph or a setback—carries within it a lesson. Through its insightful reflections, the book encourages learners and educators alike to view success and failure not as end points, but as essential milestones in the journey toward wisdom and leadership.'

—Niranjan Hiranandani,
co-founder and managing director,
Hiranandani Group

'Learning is the cradle of eternal growth and those who stop learning halt the clock of progress. This book is a compelling guide, reminding leaders that continuous learning is the true path to lasting impact and evolution. The secret to eternal youth is continuous learning.'

—Surendra Hiranandani,
founder and director, Hiranandani Group

EMPOWERMENT
—— through ——
LEARNING

KALYANI PATNAIK

**PENGUIN
ENTERPRISE**

An imprint of Penguin Random House

PENGUIN ENTERPRISE

Penguin Enterprise is an imprint of the Penguin Random House group of companies whose addresses can be found at global.penguinrandomhouse.com

Published by Penguin Random House India Pvt. Ltd
4th Floor, Capital Tower 1, MG Road,
Gurugram 122 002, Haryana, India

First published in Penguin Enterprise by Penguin Random House India 2025

ISBN 9780143477242

Typeset in Adobe Garamond Pro
Printed at Thomson Press India Ltd, New Delhi

www.penguin.co.in

Contents

Note from the Author

I owe it to my family and friends; as well as to all those near and dear, young and old, who were closely associated with me in writing this book. This book is also dedicated to all educators and learners.

Foreword

When a committed and enthusiastic educator with total dedication wants to ignite the flame of learning in young minds and decides to pen her thoughts in order to share her varied and first-hand experiences, which has manifested as a book that can be read by all—it is truly a wonderful gift to society. The thoughts expressed by her are those of a committed and sincere guru, who has had a sterling journey in the world of learning.

The book *Empowering Through Learning* written by Kalyani Patnaik—who is currently the principal of Hiranandani Foundation School, Powai—is truly a guide for people coming from all walks of life for inspiration and value in life.

As a principal, for over two decades, she has shaped and carved many lives under her watchful eyes, lives who are making positive differences to society in all spheres.

This does not come as a surprise, for here is an educator, who believes that learning is unstoppable. Kalyani madam walks the talk. She has, through her administrative sagacity and years of experience, understood the fault lines, and as a teacher, she provides the islands for respite, care, and reflection.

Further, she is committed to the ardent belief that challenges and mistakes should not stop anyone from walking the path of seeking self-actualization along with contributing to society.

In fact, Mrs Patnaik believes that it enhances grit and determination to strive and to seek beyond expectations, and to understand the various challenges that one has to face in the march of life.

It is in *Empowering Through Learning* where she explores this concept of understanding the experiences of life in an organic manner. To learn from the hard knocks of life, to seek from the trials and tribulations that one faces, and to capture learnings from every situation is her advice.

What is striking is that she does not portray a rosy picture. Through her chapters, she traverses the unique situations that are presented in front of us and how we need to relate to the positive learnings and most importantly, move on, as Chapter 8 says, 'Walk your path and go far.' She also says that there will be mistakes but as she says later in Chapter 12, 'Mistakes are also great teachers.'

This learning does not come easy. When life presents its very unpredictable situations, the natural reaction is that we cave in and give up. But Mrs Patnaik says that this is when one should script their freedom. Further, giving small anecdotes from her long career, she advises that being diplomatic is a classic way to walk on the tough road of life.

Kalyani Patnaik, in her book, through her extremely well thought out sixteen chapters whose titles are in itself so motivating, captures the various lived experiences that provide a distinct and unique perspective to handle and face situations.

It is a need of the hour that educators pen down their experiences that they have garnered over the years. This book is basically a *Path to Leadership* in a sense, as it beautifully emphasizes how to pick up the best learnings that comes one's way. It motivates us to see the opportunity to grow in any situation and not to let the negative influences tarnish the path.

The writings are a beautiful amalgamation of advice, explanations, and examples that will inspire the readers as they would be able to relate to it first-hand. The writing is lucid as Mrs Patnaik recounts her real-life experiences for her readers to learn or even be inspired by the same. It is always inspiring to read and understand how to move ahead with confidence and with a sense of conviction. Her book will provide various such anchors where the ship of the fleeting thoughts can be docked on a calm island of reflection, which will give a steady direction to sail the river of life with confidence and, most importantly, with happiness.

—Dr Radha Kumar,
professor of Ancient Indian Culture,
St Xavier's College, Mumbai

'Look deep into nature, and then you will understand everything better.'

—Albert Einstein

1

The Environment Is the Best Teacher

When the apple fell on Sir Isaac Newton's head, the gravitational theory in physics was formulated. Watching the apple fall and questioning why it fell straight down rather than sideways led to a great scientific discovery: the law of gravity. Numerous activities take place in the natural environment; one merely has to observe the environment to embark on one's learning journey.

Nature is our first teacher. We have learnt this the hard way. Wise men who abide by the rules of nature are on the right path to essential learning and findings. Learning from the environment is the most excellent experiential education one can achieve. The earth itself is the genesis and the nemesis. Any natural disruption caused by human beings has led to untold misery and sorrow. The Covid-19 pandemic has proven it all. If we had been more careful about how we wanted to progress, we should have made caring for nature a priority. It has been proven that when left alone, man fends for himself by drawing inspiration from whatever he sees in the environment.

The environment comprises the trees, animals, rivers, mountains, air, and even insects. From them we learn many important lessons that no closed classroom or technology can teach. If we observe carefully, the environment shows us how to live, grow, and care for the world we inhabit. Every aspect of nature—from the smallest seed to the tallest mountain—plays a role in shaping who we are and how we understand the world.

One of the most important lessons we learn from the environment is how everything is interconnected. All aspects of nature, like trees, rivers, animals, and even tiny insects, work together to keep the ecosystem balanced. Just like nature depends on its different parts, we are interdependent. Life would not be possible without trees to give us oxygen or rivers to give us water. This shows us that our survival depends on the health of the world around us.

Our relationship with nature is not one of separation but of interdependence. We are not mere observers of nature but integral parts of it. This understanding is crucial for maintaining an ecological balance. Our sensitivity to nature is not just a tool for self-regulation but a responsibility. This understanding should instil a deep respect and responsibility for the environment.

Understanding the Difference Between 'Environment' and 'Nature'

The 'environment' is a human construct. It's the result of our interactions with the natural world. On the other hand, 'nature' is the natural world itself, consisting of things unaffected by human technology. This distinction is critical to understanding our relationship with the world around us and how we can interact with it sustainably and respectfully.

When we talk of nature, we refer to the natural world and its components including plants, animals, landscapes, weather, and all physical entities beyond human intervention. It is in its purest form. While referring to the environment, both man-made and natural elements are included. It includes social and physical ecosystems as well as built surroundings.

Nature is limited to forests, rivers, mountains, oceans, wildlife, and natural processes (for example, the water cycle and seasons), and exists independently of human intervention. The 'environment' is a broader term that includes both natural (trees, rivers, etc.) and man-made elements (cities, buildings, pollution, etc.). There is a close relationship between living organisms like plants, animals, and humans, and their surroundings in the environment.

Nature is everything in the world that is not made by humans. It includes:

- Trees, plants, and flowers
- Animals and birds
- Rivers, oceans, and mountains
- Rain, wind, sunshine, and seasons

The environment is everything around us—both natural and human-made. It includes:

- Nature (like trees, animals, rivers)

- Things people make (like houses, roads, cars, and buildings)
- Places where we live, work, study, and play

The real difference between nature and the environment is seen in terms of their utility and diversity. One is vast and helps sustain life on Earth, while the other creates a balance between natural systems and human development.

Nature includes the sources of resources, biodiversity, and beauty which are vital for maintaining an ecological balance and for sustaining life on Earth. The environment, however, determines the quality of life for organisms. A healthy environment ensures the balance between natural systems and human development.

Nature is natural and exists as is, but the environment is created and built on nature.

Lessons from the Earth

A student watching a cloud formation while driving, considering the magnitude of sunset, seeing golden autumn leaves fall, or watching a flock of birds migrating begins to wonder what lessons the Earth can teach us. The lesson one learns from the changing seasons is that significant change is bound to happen, and that nothing is permanent. Trees do not compare themselves with one another, they only compare their growth to their previous selves. Each tree is unique. Stephen Hawking, one of the most brilliant theoretical physicists in history, explored the origins and structure of the universe—from the Big Bang to black holes—and revolutionized the field of science by relying on the universe itself to understand how it works.

Our ancestors have taught us that human existence without nature is impossible, and we owe it to nature and the environment for all the benefits enjoyed because nature is a healer. I once observed my dog searching the garden and then I found him eating leaves. I later learned that eating leaves was healing and aiding his digestion. Condors, the most fantastic bird of South America, live with dignity. When their end comes, they retreat quietly to an unknown place and drop themselves down there by surrendering to the almighty.

Andean condors are the largest raptors in the world and an absolute delight to watch in the wild. I saw one on a trip to the Andes, and my curiosity got the better of me. Reading and researching made me understand them better and I found that, being heavy, condors cannot stay airborne for long. Instead, they depend on Mother Nature—the wind—to soar to breathtaking heights. Similarly, we can also seek nature's help to reach all heights in life.

The three natural ways of leading a healthy and long life are the three Ws: Walking, Water, and Weathering odds. These elements when understood and respected can significantly enhance our quality of life and our understanding of the environment.

Walking

We all know walking is good for our health, but walking in an open, low-pollution surroundings enhances physical well-being that benefits the mind and the soul and keeps you agile. With every walk in nature, one receives far more than what they seek. If we had not walked, we would not have discovered why the squirrels come out during a particular season to hunt for nuts or why the cacophony of the crows is essential to how they transmit complex information. Walking barefoot over dew-laden grass in the morning stimulates the pressure points, helps improve the functioning of the nervous system and eyesight, and, above all, creates a feel-good factor. Therefore, it truly keeps you energized throughout the day. Walking in nature is indeed the magic potion of life.

'Stopping by Woods on a Snowy Evening' is a poem by Robert Frost. It is a thought-provoking poem packed with realizations. Despite the harsh weather, the woods are alluring, drawing one in with their darkness and all-encompassing presence. Harshness teaches us to be more polite and all-encompassing. The snow needs to be present if water is to be formed. It is the first lesson of the environment. Walking during any part of the day is a cycle of learning. We, therefore, walk not only to improve our health but also to stop and learn the lessons the environment has to share. Every step we take in nature is a step towards understanding and respecting the environment.

Spend a fortune on walking shoes; you will not regret it. You will walk miles ahead and enhance your life.

Water

Water is known as the elixir of life. It helps digest food and transport nutrients across the body, making it one of the universe's most essential elements. The fact that two-thirds of Earth is composed of water and only one-third of land is nothing short of magical. We must understand what facilitated the first life and how evolution led to more advanced life forms, including human life. We must learn from water that as much as we need it for survival, we must respect and conserve it, instilling in us a sense of responsibility and commitment.

I like what Dr Masaru Emoto mentions in the New York Times bestseller *The Hidden Messages in Water*: that there is indeed a close relationship between human consciousness and the molecular structure of water. In many traditions, water is considered sacred—often sprinkled at the start of new ventures or before joyous events as an auspicious gesture. Water is supposed to have a purifying effect, but it has some rhythm and movement in it. It is associated with wisdom and finds its way through crevices and obstacles to meet its destination—the sea. It teaches us three important lessons:

1. No journey to the attainment of a goal is simple. It needs obstacles to override and loopholes to ignore.
2. Water teaches us to flow in a musical rhythm and keep purifying ourselves.
3. Water is all-embracing; it shows that where there is a will, there is always a way.

Enjoy the spring water whenever you can, even if you are not thirsty, as springs are not found everywhere. Feel the difference and realize how energetic and rejuvenated you are.

Weather

The first contact humans have with the external environment is the moment that they are born. The first lesson, therefore, is to weather the external force. Weathering the storm is a common ideology for all those who want to overcome difficulties in life. The more obstacles you encounter, the stronger you get. Learning together about the storms in your life helps you not only survive the most challenging times but also grow from them.

Mark Twain once said, 'Climate is what we expect; weather is what we get.' Modern society is spoilt for choice and today's students are brilliant but have not learned to manage their thoughts properly. Harnessing all positive thoughts and enduring tough ones is like the weathering process of nature. The word 'weather' itself is a mnemonic for three powerful elements of the universe: water, earth, and ether. Therefore, we learn from the weather to overcome troubles, become more robust, and evolve and set new goals. The sky is limitless.

Take an umbrella with holes and go out on a rainy day. You have weathered the force of adversities and strengthened your life's journey. So, the learnings from the environment would be:

Walk to explore
Water to nurture
Weather for strength

For me, the lessons from the environment have been manifold:

1. Learn to respect the environment.
2. Never encroach upon territories that do not belong to you.
3. Each living being has a purpose and a goal—trees, birds, and even the tiniest of ants. Therefore, we need to respect all.
4. Earth is our *Pachamama* (Mother Earth). Never let it bleed, or it can be very costly for the succeeding generation.

5. Trees, shrubs, flora, and fauna are the Earth's lungs. They must never be depleted, or we will soon be asphyxiated.
6. We must serve and protect nature as it is the only wealth of humanity.

'Cherish the natural world, because you're a part of it and you depend on it.'

—David Attenborough

* * *

My learnings from nature have developed my intuition, which has helped guide me further. As American virologist and researcher Jonas Salk mentions, 'It is always with excitement that I wake up in the morning, wondering what my intuition will toss at me like gifts from the sea. I work with it and rely on it. It's my partner'. We must protect the environment and treat it as a responsibility rather than just a duty. The lessons we learn from the environment are often the ones that stay with us the longest.

We are learning from the seasons. We know nothing is permanent or infallible. We learn impermanence from seasons, they teach us that glory can be achieved only after facing a cycle of storm and strife. One can learn a lot from observing a tree and impart that learning to young students. For me, the three Rs are so important. The tree also teaches you the same three Rs—aRithmetic, Reading, and wRiting.

The ones important to me are—Resilience, Resoluteness, and Rootedness.

Resilience empowers one to deal with difficult situations peacefully. The power of being resilient enhances the following:

1. Academic success: Enhances perseverance and coping mechanisms, reducing exam stress and improving performance.
2. Social well-being: Improves empathy, conflict resolution, and ability to manage social pressures.
3. Personal growth: Boosts self-confidence, mental health, adaptability, and outlook on life.

Being resolute empowers one to tackle any conflicting situation. We often encounter situations that involve conflict, of interest. Every leader has to learn how to avoid such situations by being firm and not getting lulled by smooth and sweet talking.

Being rooted in firm, value-related beliefs keep one grounded in schedules and discipline. It helps one connect to their inner self. Storms of nature form deep roots.

> 'In nature, nothing is perfect. Trees can be contorted, bent weirdly, and still beautiful.'
>
> —Alice Walker

* * *

Nurture Nature

We have to nurture nature if we wish to show love and respect for the environment that sustains all life on Earth. This includes protecting our great forests, shielding our rivers against pollutants and preserving the wildlife.

Nature gives us clean air, fresh water, food, and beauty, but it cannot care for itself. When we plant trees, we in turn reduce waste, conserve energy, and protect animals.

Nurturing nature is not just about big actions; even small, mindful choices like switching off lights, saying no to plastic, or growing a plant in the back yard of your home can make a huge difference. By caring for nature today, we ensure a healthier, safer, and more beautiful world for the future generations.

Practices and Projects

1. Good environmental practices: There should be a five-bin segregation system under the following categories:
   i. Metal waste
   ii. Plastic waste
   iii. Electronic waste (e-waste)
   iv. Paper waste
   v. Glass waste
2. Conservation of Water: Consume water wisely and according to need. Xeriscaping in drought-ridden areas and learning to harvest rainwater are useful practices.
3. Walking or carpooling to save fuel and reduce carbon footprints.
4. Organizing environment-friendly parties at home and in hotels—call it a green party day.

I will walk beside you and be your friend.

2

Friends and Learnings

No man is an island, and likewise, no country can thrive in isolation. Friends make it easier for humans to exist and progress. Friends can be of myriad kinds, and each has a story to tell, leaving behind a golden lesson. In the earlier chapter, I discussed the environment as one of the most outstanding teachers of humanity. Although these teachings may be intangible, they have great, profound wisdom that humans can learn from. After all, we *Homo sapiens* are quick learners. If the environment is the greatest teacher, then friends are the most significant influencers. They are the ones who endorse the lessons, and this becomes learning.

Friendships can be between humans or between species. The rules of friendship depend on many factors, but nothing progresses without the regulations of A, B, C, and D.

A: Affection expressed through sharing and learning brings friends together. Affection can be in many forms, and it can be demonstrated positively between individuals. It is one emotion that is highly necessary when weaving people together as it fosters connection and understanding. It may be in the form of good, respectful writing with positive words or it may also be by lending your ear to others' point of view.

Helping and sharing are some ways of showing affection. In other words, affection can be shown by taking care.

B: Bonding follows when you start living with one another. Most captives are moved from prison to prison as bonds between cellmates emerge within the span of a year.

Your schoolmates and college mates are your best buddies. These bonds are so strong that you would be able to pick up where you left off even if you haven't been in touch for years. Reminiscing about the past, networking, and then staying in touch are phrases best practiced.

C: Communication between people is no longer a problem today. Staying in contact and communicating positively can affect a friendship significantly. Covid-19 has been instrumental in teaching us that true friendship can transcend physical barriers. Communication through connection has contributed immensely to excellent or bad friendships.

D: Dependability built on trust and faith goes a long way. Friendships last for eternity. Great nations support one another once trust and faith develops between them. At times of crisis, we know whom to depend upon. Built upon the aforementioned parameters, friendship relies on the golden rule of ABCD. The rest follows.

Different types of friendships teach us different lessons. In an article for *Psychology Today*, Dr Mariana Bockarova notes that a person's behaviour and character are shaped by the kind of friends they keep. Charles Darwin said, 'A man's friendships are one of the best measures of his worth'. It sums up that one can learn from one's friends. One is shaped by those around them, and one needs to understand friendship through the eyes of those around them. Friendship should be characterized by strong respect and trust. One can categorize friendship based on Aristotle's *Nicomachean Ethics*, which is as follows:

1. Friendship of utility
2. Friendship of pleasure
3. Friendship of values

The friendship of utility is businesslike, and people learn to respect each other as long as the business between the two individuals lasts. The next type of friendship lasts as long as one enjoys each other's company. The friendship based on values is the friendship of goodness. By nature, everyone wants to be good, admired, and respected. This type of friendship brings a lot of learning.

When someone asks me why I like writing, I only say that penning down my thoughts makes me feel empowered. However, I was motivated by a school friend of mine. Every time I discovered her essays were better than mine, I would force myself to improve until, one day, writing became a passion. What life lessons can we learn from friends? They can be summarised as follows:

1. Transferable skills: These learning strategies are predicated upon getting involved in a friendship group. We learn to collaborate, be empathetic, read emotions, and regulate aggression.
2. Learning to take risks: If I were to scale Mount Everest for the first time, I'd never venture out alone. Even Edmund Hillary climbed it with Tenzing Norgay and learnt the art of risk-taking from his friends.
3. Collaborative learning: All individuals, no matter how accomplished, learn only by collaborating with others who may have bigger ideas that can hone one's skills further.

Friends are an important part of our lives. Friends are more than just companions; they are our teachers. In life, we meet different friends who help us and teach us valuable lessons. They teach us life skills and give us support during tough times, helping us grow as people.

Friends in Personal Growth

One of the most significant ways that friends contribute to our learning is by encouraging personal growth. True friends challenge us to become better versions of ourselves. They encourage us to pursue our goals and help us stay on track when we face obstacles. Often, it is because of their guidance and constructive criticism that we are able to see ourselves more clearly, recognize our strengths, and work on our weaknesses.

We find ourselves motivated to achieve goals because we have friends who believe in us. Whether it's succeeding in school, advancing our careers, or simply being a better person, friends provide the encouragement and support needed to keep going. They remind us of our potential, especially when we lose confidence in ourselves.

We learn through shared experience. Working on group projects or tackling challenges together allows us to learn new skills such as teamwork, problem-solving, and time management. These shared experiences teach us how to collaborate effectively and work towards a common goal. Often, we realize that we learn as much from our friends' ways of thinking as we do from the task at hand. We discover each other's talents.

Friends are also our emotional teachers. They show us the importance of trust. Through their actions, we learn how to be supportive and how to care for others. During times of emotional turmoil, friends provide comfort and understanding. They teach us how to be strong in the face of adversity and how to process difficult emotions in healthy ways.

One of the most valuable lessons friends teach us is the importance of diversity. Friends come from various backgrounds, and through them, we gain insight into different cultures, traditions, and ways of thinking. This diversity helps us become more open-minded. When we spend time with friends from different cultures or backgrounds, we learn to respect their views, even if they differ from our own.

Diverse friendships also teach us tolerance and the ability to compromise. We might not always agree with our friends, but by talking respectfully and being open-minded, we learn to handle these differences and make our friendships stronger. Interacting with different people helps us become more flexible, understanding, and caring.

Therefore, friends are more than just people we spend time with; they are important teachers who help us grow and learn. Through our friendships, we become better individuals by sharing experiences, offering support, and learning from each other. Friends help us build stronger relationships and give us the strength to handle life's challenges. The lessons we learn from them stay with us, helping us become kinder, wiser, and more caring. Friendship is not just about having fun together but also about growing and becoming the best version of ourselves. *Hitopadesha* and *Aesop's Fables* are full of morals and explicitly address the values of friendship. Stories like 'The Fox and the Grapes' depict the inner nature of humanity and how it is so easy to despise something we don't have, but the inner truth is that we have to accept what we cannot change and learn to be content with what we have. I enjoy the story 'The Bear and the Two Friends' in which one of the friends runs away and climbs a tree upon seeing the bear. The friend who doesn't know how to climb trees quietly lies down on the ground, and the bear, after sniffing him, goes away. The lesson learnt by these two friends is that true friends will not desert you in times of need.

An oft-repeated war story about unconditional friendship is worth mentioning here. Two best buddies, Harry and Bill, were classmates from kindergarten through their college days. When the war broke out, they joined the army and asked to be in the same unit. While on patrol one night, they were ambushed, and bullets started flying from all sides. Out of the darkness, Harry recognized Bill's voice calling out for help. Harry asked his Captain to help his best friend, but he declined. He kept quiet and heard Bill's voice again. Harry couldn't do anything as he heard Bill's voice repeatedly on the battlefield. He couldn't contain himself any longer, so Harry ran over to his Captain again, who reluctantly agreed to let him go. Through the darkness, Harry crawled and dragged Bill back to their camp, where he was declared dead. Furious, the Captain shouted at Harry and told him that going out there was a mistake, and that he could've died. The moral of this story is that a friend, dead or alive, is still a friend. The strong connection of friendship allowed him to take a risk.

The principles of DIET (**D**ependability, **I**ntegrity, **E**mpathy, **T**rust), when followed, lay the foundations for a strong and healthy friendship. Great friendships bring in great learnings which in turn results in better understanding between two individuals. This makes the friendship more robust.

Friendship, does not have an age barrier. It goes beyond making friends with human beings. It is built on DIET, which needs to be maintained under all circumstances.

I like what Muhammad Ali had to say about friendship: 'Friendship is the hardest thing in the world to explain. It is not something you learn in school, but if you haven't learned the meaning of friendship, you haven't learned anything'. True friendship begins with learnings that grow into deeper understanding, and this understanding makes friendship more robust and meaningful for our existence.

The art of making friends is all about learning the techniques of a relationship. People from prominent communities and families make friends faster than those who are more reserved and have had very little exposure to sports or other social activities. Here's a story that clarifies how one must use their strengths and techniques to make friends.

There was once a boy called Smaran who joined Class 8 in a new school. He was short and puny, and the students made fun of him by jeering at him whenever he tried to do something new. He was hurt and could not share his woes with anybody. He didn't want to talk to his parents about it, fearing that it would upset them, and the teacher worried he wouldn't be heard. While he tried sharing his food and followed various other methods to build bridges, it only earned him a couple of well-wishers and a few short-lived friends. One day, the school announced an inter-house swimming competition, and the house captain went around taking down names. Smaran was an excellent swimmer, and this opportunity allowed him to showcase his skills. He was very excited that the school was conducting a competition of this kind. He learnt how to swim from his grandfather, who also taught him some lessons about life through swimming. Whenever he went on holiday to his village in Punjab, he practiced the art of swimming, and tried to swim across small ponds as per his father and grandfather's guidance. Consequently, he developed a passion for it. He continued to hone the art of swimming by going to the pool every weekend. Just as Smaran was about to give his name to the school's house captain, the entire class screamed in unison, demanding that he first show the medal he had already won. Summoning his courage, Smaran stepped forward and said to the captain, 'Give me another chance. I won't just win a trophy for our house—I'll bring home several medals'. He wanted to participate in the competitions for which he was registered. The day of the competition arrived, and lo and behold, a spectacular sight was seen—he swam like a fish gliding through the water, occasionally popping up like a dolphin. His housemasters were overjoyed and started shouting with glee. They looked rapt by his agility and speed. Smaran turned a deaf ear to these shouts and only focused on the prize. He wanted to enjoy the water and concentrated only on the trophy. When he reached the finish line, he realized that his competitors were far behind, and that he had won. He came out of the pool, lifted a great trophy and with it, earned a wave of admiration that won him many friends. He earned his friends through his sheer strength and talent.

Friends are also made when you extend a helping hand. You win friends easily through acts of kindness and by sharing your joy and feelings. Therefore, we must understand that friendship cannot be taught through definite training.

It is an art that can only be self-developed. As I mentioned in my previous book, *The Path to Leadership*, identifying and leveraging one's strengths helps us win friends.

One of the most common parables we grew up with is 'The Lion and the Mouse' from *Aesop's Fables*. The lion always believed it was the mightiest because of its size, while the mouse, being much smaller, was seen as weak. As the story goes, when the lion was caught in a net by a hunter, it was the mouse, however small it may be, that could set the lion free. It nibbled at the net and created an exit for the lion. While the story speaks of friendship, what struck me the most was this: perhaps it was an act of kindness being repaid. To me, the essence of the story is this—your kindness reminded me to be kinder. Help, compassion, and love have to be unconditional. Kindness begets kindness. We all know that a mother's love and the love between siblings is unconditional and forever bonding. What exactly is unconditional love between friends?

1. Unconditional love between friends means willing to go to any extent to help a friend in times of need, regardless of whether they've helped you in return.
2. Friends understand each other's views and respect any differences that may exist between them.
3. You don't expect anything in return when you help someone. Empathy is unconditional love.

Such friends are true and dependable. Animals, perhaps, are another fine example of best buddies. A dog is considered faithful because it offers unconditional love. Another story that captures the meaning of good friendship is a personal favourite of mine—*The Jungle Book*. Though fictitious, it speaks of beautiful relationships between animals and humans, showing how friendship transcends all boundaries of caste, creed, and gender. The little boy Mowgli grew up only in the company of animals. His best friends, Baloo, the bear, and Bagheera, the black panther, had to bribe the pack of wolves to care for Mowgli. All fictitious stories have great lessons about friendship and being with one another. Amidst all the chaos, anger, bitterness and competition in today's world, it is imperative that our relationships be built on a positive foundation. We have forgotten that no situation will remain the same forever. Thus, friends are necessary to walk the path with you.

Elevate your company of friends and elevate the 'U' in you.

Practices and Projects

If friendship enriches your life, then learning to develop friendship goals is important. Here are a few tips for establishing good friendships and relationships:

1. Be a good listener during a conversation. Tell yourself that you will spend ten minutes simply listening and twenty minutes in which you will neither interrupt nor add any words.
2. Respect each other's confidentiality. You don't have to pour your heart out, but if you do, respect for trust and privacy is a must.
3. Test the waters of friendship. To test true friendship, observe how your friends behave in situations and how they respond to each other's needs. True friends are reciprocative and consistent in words and deeds.
4. Nothing should be expected in return—friendship is unconditional.
5. Finally, if you are physically not around, you must be available for advice and help.

* * *

Identify the difference between networking and friendship:

1. Friendship plays a significant role—it is permanent and precious. Networking, on the other hand, is for sharing resources and values. If it goes beyond this, it becomes friendship; otherwise, it dissolves into a mere acquaintance. Some tips for developing resilience and toleration for all kinds of friendship are:
   i. Exercising trust and transaction helps you identify good friends. There is no harm in having fair-weather friends but it's also important to have boundaries. Building emotional well-being can be a powerful tool to help

you withstand and tolerate all kinds of people. Practice stillness of mind through meditation.

ii. Declutter your minds and say 'done and dusted' once the friendship ends.

Pursue a hobby and do not let emotions rule you.

Some of my favourite films about friendship are:

1. *Sholay* (1975)
2. *The Bucket List* (2007)
3. *The Intouchables* (2011)
4. *Duma* (2005)

Sometimes, animals can be your friends. They bond and understand like humans do, and you can learn great things from them as well.

Cheering is an action rebound theory.

3

Be Your Own Cheerleader

It's not about being the best but being better than you were yesterday. 'The unselfish effort to bring cheer to others will be the beginning of a happier life for ourselves.' This quote by Helen Keller brings out a clear difference between cheering and cheerleaders.

Cheering is for joy. Cheerleaders are those who learn to cheer teams and are physically present on the sports ground when competitive events or other functions are held. This chapter provides tips on how to cheer oneself and keep the spirits high. Cheerleading is a routine backed by payment and incentives. At the same time, being a cheerleader brings immense satisfaction and joy, which is more significant than any other work.

Be your own cheerleader. Life's journey is not a straight line but a meandering river filled with challenges. In today's world, we are often overwhelmed by gadgets, gizmos, and ambitions, leaving little time for self-reflection. However, by embracing self-cheering, we can navigate life's obstacles with resilience and positivity, leading to a more fulfilling and joyful existence.

In a dynamic world, we are all busy and driven by great expectations. In the bargain, we often forget about ourselves; we love to cheer others, but how often do we choose to cheer ourselves?

It is very important that we recognize our hard work and progress. This helps us understand the concept of self-compassion and the importance of treating ourselves with the same kindness and support that we offer others. We should try to give others the kind of gift we would want for ourselves. This creates a healthy environment between individuals.

Being positive can sometimes help one's mental health and make people feel better about themselves. However, mental health is an infinitely more nuanced topic, and I would encourage seeking support from a mental health professional if you are struggling with your mental health. Talking about one's emotions and experiences makes one more resilient as it requires a lot of courage to seek help. It also helps one deal with their problems in a healthier manner.

I remember a student who wasn't given a position on the student council and all that he said was, 'I expected to be a house captain, but never mind. I will do better, and I will earn a position next year.' This way of thinking helps one view setbacks as opportunities to grow, rather than as reasons to give up. Being your own cheerleader also means giving yourself credit. So what if no one praises you? A good feeling develops when you feel satisfied, look out for yourself and upscale when needed.

Self-cheering has many psychological benefits. The way you treat yourself affects how you relate to others and helps you connect with people even better. It also helps boost self-efficacy. I believe that one can control their life when they believe in themselves—we are more likely to take actions and make things happen.

There are very simple ways to cheer yourself:

1. Practice positive self-talk—this will remind you to be positive and make you stronger. It will help you develop great willpower.
2. Every small win should be celebrated as though it were a bigger achievement—these little celebrations become stepping stones to greater confidence.
3. Setting goals is something that always helps boost the right kind of confidence and motivation.
4. We do our best when we create a positive circle filled with supportive people instead of critical ones—the mantra is to stay away from toxic company.
5. Finally, imagine that success is yours and that your goals are within reach. Sometimes, this really helps, and you start believing in yourself even more.

Most people are too harsh on themselves because they are perfectionists, and being a perfectionist can only make you feel like you are never enough. This can sometimes lead to a lot of negative thoughts, and we must replace them with positive ones. Therefore, learning to show kindness to yourself is a very powerful act of self-care, that leads to a more meaningful and fulfilling life, so learn to cheer yourself.

Below is a beautiful story about cheering yourself up:

Once, a man had a terrible day. Everything seemed to go wrong, and he was filled with negative emotions. He didn't know how to snap out of it. This continued for several days. He joined a group that had a leader, teachers, and entrepreneurs.

One day, the man learned that he could control his thoughts and emotions. He started practising self-care and discovered activities that brought him joy and positivity. He learned to meditate, exercise regularly, and surrounded himself with positive people. He also found that expressing gratitude helped shift his perspective and focus on the good things in life. He made it a habit to write down three things he was thankful for every day.

Over time, the man learned to turn the terrible days into good ones by practising various techniques of *pranayama*, a practice in yoga, playing chess, and focusing on the things that made him and the people around him happy. He soon realized that he was in control of his happiness and that no external situation could take that away. He continued to grow and develop coping skills, and eventually, the bad days became fewer. He eventually learned that with effort and practice, one could change their outlook and find joy in life, no matter what obstacles one encounters.

The next time he played a game of chess—which he lost after several rounds of winning earlier—he shook hands with his opponent and cheered him on as the greatest of the winners. The winner responded humbly. These reciprocated cheers only made him feel more elated.

* * *

There was once a school's annual award ceremony to which only the prize winners and their parents were invited. Subsequent meetings raised the question of why those who didn't win any awards were not invited. The answer was: why should they even be called if they were not receiving anything? I suggested calling the non-prize winners to teach them how to clap for others—otherwise they will never appreciate anyone's achievements in life. They would be raised with the strong conviction that felicitation ceremonies need no audience, and thus miss the opportunity to learn from others' successes.

Leaders need to teach their teams to clap for others. Putting both hands together ensures meaningful learning and leads to resounding personal success. It's no wonder the best approach is to embrace every situation and appreciate everything. The power of positivity broadens one's perspective of life, contributing to overall well being. If no one claps for you, learn to clap for yourself and for every effort you make. You must remember that when you appreciate your work and decide to improve, you will get better.

When is it that we do not cheer for others? It only happens in two situations: first, when we are too awestruck by admiration and second, when we are too envious. In the first case, the admiration is continuous—it leads to inspiration, motivation, and emulation. For example, you may become a good writer when you read a prize-winning book that inspires you to write more. Working towards inspiration leads to motivation, and cheering others on leads to creation. This is the power of learning from others—it's about being open-minded and receptive to the lessons they can teach us.

The inability to cheer people on is often seen as a burden that weighs heavily on the mind, eventually transforming a person into a loner.

Athletes fight their own battles with their competitors on the field. The one who doesn't win always congratulates the winner and learns from their winning traits to improve themselves further. This is called self-cheering.

There are numerous great self-cheering techniques. For instance, make a list of only ten things to work on within a year and start fulfilling them.

1. I love dancing in the rain as no one can see my tears.
2. I love wearing dresses that look good on someone else. So what if they don't look good on me? I still love them.
3. I like to sing, and even though I cannot, I will still record it and keep it for myself.
4. Writing for pleasure, not for publishing.
5. Invent a new game.

There are endless self-cheering moments waiting to be invented.

Alexander and the Terrible, Horrible, No Good, Very Bad Day by Judith Viorst is a heartwarming book that appreciates the good things in life despite a series of hardships.

Challenge the negative thoughts by engaging in activities that bring you joy. Make your hardships feel lighter and let the difficult times fly by. You can keep your spirits high by following the mantra of returning to school to learn a new skill. You can enroll in any of the following schools, which cater to the following:

1. A school that has newer degrees like cooking, carpentry or painting.
2. A school that engages with the natural environment through trekking in mountains, hills and even plains.
3. A school that wants to be engaged with the young and underprivileged.

Learning from the above strengthens your indomitable spirit as you learn to cheer yourself up. Once you know how to cheer yourself up, you will also become skilled at cheering others.

Let us, before the day ends, say that we are grateful for the day that has passed. So, we say CHEERS by raising:

A **C**upful of **H**eartfelt gratitude for an **E**xciting, **E**ncouraging, **R**adiant and **S**afe day.

The next day, with the rising sun, will bring new hopes and even greater learnings.

How to Cheer Others

Three steps to becoming a stalwart at cheering others:

1. Attend celebrations of the successes of juniors or colleagues younger than yourself. It is often easiest to cheer them the loudest. The outcome will be gaining new ideas from the younger generation, which adds to your existing knowledge and learning.

2. Next, attend award ceremonies honouring seniors, such as inspiring leaders who have made an indelible mark. Cheer the loudest for them, as you will feel motivated, inspired and overwhelmed with joy.

3. Finally, when you visit a peer or competitor and face an opponent who has won, you will find that you know exactly how to congratulate them. Your takeaway here is to put yourself and your ego last, and to be happy for the achievements of others. This helps you build resilience. When you cheer someone who has done better than you, you learn to compete with yourself. In this way, you earn respect, develop maturity, and gain goodwill.

How Do You Cheer Yourself?

Develop the calmness of your power and meditate on your achievements. This will help you see the path ahead more clearly and become the first step toward getting back on track.

Here are some beautiful phrases that bring about good cheer:

1. Practice creates confidence. Keep trying, and you shall succeed.
2. Bravo, only you could have done it.
3. Want to win, and the battle is won.

How do we toast and say 'Cheers'?

This is done by raising a glass of wine or any drink and saying the phrase 'Cheers!'—toasting to health, happiness, or success.

'Be of good cheer. Do not think of today's failures, but of the success that may come tomorrow. You have set yourselves a difficult task, but you will succeed if you persevere; and you will find a joy in overcoming obstacles. Remember, no effort that we make to attain something beautiful is ever lost.'

—Helen Keller

At regular intervals, measure the goals you have achieved and move on to the next until all are accomplished. This is true cheering—whether for yourself or a group working toward their goals.

1. Enhance your joy by surrounding yourself with the laughter and cheer of family members. Carry that warmth with you and spread it wherever you go.
2. Start a cheering club based on the principles of purpose, aim, and interest, and promote it.

Cheer and steer your path to becoming an empowered leader.

Dreaming and setting goals predict a bright future.

4

Learning to Dream and Setting Goals

'The path from dreams to success does exist. May you have the vision to find it, the courage to get on to it, and the perseverance to follow it.'

—Kalpana Chawla

Could Kalpana Chawla have soared into the sky of success if she had not dared to dream that there was an entire universe of space to conquer?

She had a dream and specific goals regarding the conquest of space, and the vision to find the path to success through courage and perseverance.

What Does Dreaming Mean?

Dreaming focuses on an idea that strengthens your energy and tells you that realization is possible. Unfortunately, many of us are fickle-minded and struggle to focus our thoughts. We must learn to concentrate on a particular idea and make it our dream. We would never have gained freedom if our freedom fighters had not gathered and focused on the dream of seeing a free India. Martin Luther King Jr had a dream of transforming his nation into an oasis of freedom and justice. Dreams are thoughts, and goals are the realization of those thoughts. Dreams can be anything imagined the mind, but when they are rooted in goals, taking action towards realizing those goals becomes easier. Watching the environment around me— which has been an excellent teacher— has enabled me to dream and set goals.

I know a beautiful story of a shepherd boy sent to the town by his father to study engineering and improve his quality of life. Unfortunately, he failed and had to return to the forest to tend to the sheep. It was a significant blow to the family, as they had spent their entire income on his education. The young shepherd was naturally dejected and tried to identify his strengths by learning from the forest—its abundance and its challenges. He was good at overcoming obstacles, which encouraged him to advance his knowledge of the environment and forests. This passion eventually became a dream which was fulfilled by earning a career in the Indian Forest Service.

It is the pure synchrony of thoughts, dreams, and realization.

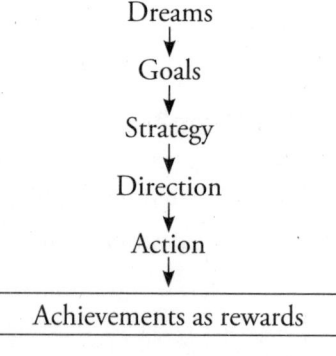

Dreams
↓
Goals
↓
Strategy
↓
Direction
↓
Action
↓

| Achievements as rewards |

1. Dreams are desires that seek realization. No one should get dejected by rejections at the start. In fact, it is better that one is rejected in the beginning because, at this point, the willingness and energy are still high, allowing one to manage stress while simultaneously improving themselves. Michael Jordan, is a great example of this. He once commented, 'I've missed more than 9,000 shots in my career. I've lost almost 300 games. Twenty-six times I've been trusted to take the game-winning shot and missed. I've failed over and over and over again in my life. And that is why I succeed.' Developing a strong mindset propels progress, which was exactly why Michael Jordan won the hearts of people and the game. One dreams and then develops the courage and resilience to fulfil it.

2. Goals are aspirations aimed at lasting success. Steps must be taken toward them, not only to set effective goals. Aligning each achievement with the fulfillment of a dream becomes the true purpose. It is always better to set short-term goals before setting larger ones, as this helps build momentum towards achieving the desired outcomes. Aspirational goals can be transformed into smart goals for better and smoother results, incorporating deadlines, purposes, and progress.

3. Strategies are about planning a path to achieve a goal. Dreams can be of any kind, but without a clear vision of the road ahead, they can vanish into thin air.

4. No strategy can be fruitful unless there is direction, either from within or from outside. For me, a role model often serves to provide that direction.

5. Finally, swift action to all the above can bring complete rewards. The success and value of any action depend on the strength of the actions plans. Every action plan needs to incorporate clear timelines and a progress-tracking strategy. I know of a few leaders who only love delegating but lack the skill to follow up and expect the action to manage itself. Tracking ensures the smooth running of the organisation, as immediate corrections can be made as and when they arise.

Owing to the depth of the images formed in the mind, you will constantly work on manifesting them into reality. However, if you still do not succeed, you might allow those images to entertain you through the day, leading you to indulge in daydreaming and laziness.

What are the most useful tips for learning how to dream?

1. First, tell yourself: the impossible can be made possible. Very often, our dreams fade away. Every child in kindergarten I interact with dreams of being a service provider, like a fire officer, police officer, or teacher. However, this dream should not be viewed as literally becoming one of them, the nurturing could guide them towards a similar kind of role or service. We are often told how difficult it is to fulfil specific dreams, but are rarely told that there are tools and a design for every dream, and that we can design them.
2. Learn to design your dreams: I came across someone in college who loved teaching and uniforms but was worried that a teacher's job would not offer reasonable remuneration. Well, sometimes reinforcement is necessary

to drive passion, but one can design the dream. My friend had a passion for teaching and a love of uniforms. Today, he is a military officer in the Army Education Corps, teaching young cadets at military colleges. A dream truly designed and fulfilled.

3. Learn to use your imagination: imagination helps us visualize what we aspire to achieve by creating a mental image through which we can channel our actions. For example, someone who desires to become a helicopter pilot might first form a mental picture of themselves flying a chopper and helping ferry people during floods. While imagination and dreams are distinct concepts, they are closely related, as both involve the creation of mental images.

4. Motivate yourself to dream big: our goals are achieved only when there is a strong drive and motivation. A powerful example is when you have a dream role model who inspires you. In 2008, Joseph Schooling met his hero, Michael Phelps, and was deeply motivated. In 2016, he went on to beat his hero. The vision of the future must excite you. Many of us have goals, but we often lack the motivation to pursue them fully. A tea seller at a railway station motivates himself by aiming to earn through the good sale of tea. Each day, he strives to innovate newer and better-quality teas to achieve that goal.

In a nutshell, we can say—if you want something connected to the feelings of your dreams and goals:

1. Start by formulating a life statement. For example:
    i.   I dream of owning a factory, and working towards starting one becomes the action that brings my dream to life.

ii. I want to be an astronaut and a voracious science-fiction reader.

2. Secondly, make use of the three tools that will help you stay consistently motivated: having a clear vision, writing down your goals, and setting deadlines and milestones.

What makes a goal achievable? The word *achievable* itself. But what needs to be kept in mind is the following, which is captured by the acronym: ACHIEVABLE.

1. Aspire to achieve the goal first. Aspire to persevere confidently, continuously nurture hope and harbour optimism, identify your strengths, and discover the 'I' in you.
2. Continue to pursue your aspirations rigorously, and never quit.
3. Harbour optimism and hope to bring about the best results in whatever you do.
4. Identify your strengths and prioritize them by upskilling, and move steadily towards achieving your goals.
5. Elevate yourself by uplifting those around you. This will ease your journey and help you reach your goals more effectively.
6. The vision and goals must always be kept in mind and remain aligned on the journey to success. The vision should be reviewed and revised regularly, with an attitude aimed at reaching new heights.
7. Attitude should always support the mission of attaining greater heights.
8. Believe in yourself and always be confident. Never let overconfidence destroy you.

9. Lead a team, because you cannot achieve success alone.
10. Enjoy every moment, and remind yourself that the light at the end of the tunnel is visible.

Here's a beautiful story of a dream set on goals and vision:

While on holiday in Bhutan, I came across a town whose culture enchanted me. Their traditions and customs were something we could all to learn from. The local garb was so unique and wonderful that the men looked like knights. Their attire, called the '*gho*' is a knee-length robe wrapped around the body and neatly secured with a belt. Most striking, however, is the women's dress known as the '*kira*', which every Bhutanese woman takes pride in wearing. I had the good fortune of visiting a weaver's den, where a group of artisans were focused on crafting a bridal dress for an upcoming royal wedding. I could see a goal, a vision, and all the parameters mentioned above reflected in the weaving of the attire.

Each person had a role to play, and the leader, while directing, was also actively engaged in the work. Leaders often dream but fail to achieve their objectives because delegation lacks proper supervision. Supervision can be carried out without micromanaging and by staying alert and involved in the mission. I was told that each *kira* woven took between three to six months to complete. A *kira* that needed to be even more intricately and artistically woven, such as one for a bride, could take up to a year to complete. I definitely could not stay until the entire *kira* was woven. However, the weaver showed me a picture of a completed *kira*, which stands as a perfect example of achievement and hard work.

Practice Turning Dreams Into Goals

1. Plan a bridge that can turn your dreams into achievable goals.
2. Use the SMART criteria (Specific Measurable Attainable and Relevant and Time-bound) to guide you in building a bridge through careful planning, organization and action.
3. Always write down your dreams, keep them positive and achievable.

Dreams are dormant; they need to be activated and transformed action.

* * *

A stonecutter's dream of constructing a temple could be fulfilled only through faith, perseverance, and the power of action. His first step was to sincerely cut the first stone and begin chiseling it, and he did not stopped until the dream of the temple became a reality. The moment the first step is taken, the universe conspires to help. This is the true power of action.

It is said dreams are like bamboo seeds. They don't grow overnight. They require consistent action and continuous nurturing before the shoots emerge. More than anything, patience is what helps dreams come true. Just as bamboo roots grow unseen beneath the soil, your efforts lay the foundation for dreams to flourish.

The only gap that exists between dreaming and action is a lack of effort.

We have to be brave enough to dare to dream.

Everything you need to succeed is already within you: all that's needed is the driving force of action to make it happen.

Conclusion

We dream like countless stars in the sky, and they continue to grow until one shines brightly, signifying that a dream has been fulfilled. All dreams are kept alive by vision, effort, determination, and dedication. Like stars, dreams don't disappear; they continue to gleam even after the night is over.

Change is not the only constant. We need to evolve.

5

Learning to Upskill and Grow

It is possible to fly without motors, but not without knowledge and skill. With changing technology and the evolutionary process, staying relevant in modern times requires continuous upskilling. Someone once asked me about the need to to upskill yourself. I answered, 'Don't we want to learn how to surmount any uphill task? Continuous learning empowers us to conquer any challenge that comes our way.'

Before we delve deep into the necessity of upskilling, it's important to understand the subtle difference between upskilling and upscaling, which are often erroneously used as synonyms. Upskilling refers to progression and growth, while upscaling refers to expanding an existing parameter or phenomenon.

Perhaps the best example of upscaling today is the ability to convert an image or video to a higher-resolution format than the original. It is merely an expansion and stretching of what already exists. Reskilling, on the other hand, refers to the process of acquiring a new set of skills, enabling an individual to carry out different tasks. It may also reduce the unemployment rate.

Why are upskilling and reskilling essential, and why must we learn them?

1. Some jobs may become obsolete. If we have never learned to multitask or learn new skills, our employability value may be reduced to zero.

   Example: During the Covid-19 era, the most valuable asset was the ability to upskill by learning new IT skills that facilitated effective communication and kept jobs on track. While job security remained steady for some, the mobility of labour was severely affected.

   A carpenter, for instance, lost his job because he was no longer allowed to visit homes. Instead of giving up, he began crafting wooden toys which he then sold online. This is a prime example of how reskilling allows one to adapt to changing circumstances.

2. Reskilling leads to multitasking and ensures that one never becomes redundant: upskilling fosters qualitative growth and self-advancement.

3. Learning, upskilling, and reskilling help you become more adaptable to changing situations by adjusting to new realities. This adaptability nurtured through continuous learning makes us resilient in the face of change.

4. Learning skills from nature. Nature is a challenging taskmaster, yet a gentle teacher.

   a. Nature restores children's attention span: A walk in the garden or following a nature trail amidst thirst-quenching springs and beautiful flora not only helps relieve stress but also helps strengthen concentration skills.

b. A sound mind can reside only in a sound body: *Mens sana in corpore sano.* Physical fitness enhances mental abilities. Outdoor sports can be exhilarating. Yoga and deep breathing exercises often introduce new lifestyle skills into an individual's life.

c. Nature has long been the best trainer for innovative skills. A good example is the story of *Robinson Crusoe* by Daniel Defoe. The novel *Robinson Crusoe* proves that survival is rooted in pure determination. Great lessons come from observation and presence of mind. The novel shows us how we can increase our chances of survival by bettering ourselves little by little every day. The protagonist survives by upskilling himself each day on a deserted island and learns the profound lesson: 'All our discontents about what we want appeared to spring from the want of thankfulness for what we have'.

d. Nature helps in developing observation skills. In other words, these skills allow you to listen with more than just your ears and make better decisions. To develop your critical thinking skills, always: (i) look outwards, (ii) remove distractions, (iii) recall, and (iv) analyse.

Why Is a Skill an Asset?

A skill is more than an asset; it can be as a saving grace. My son, who is a computer engineer, had to stay live abroad alone for several years, and his cooking skills became a saving grace.

He never had to depend on food from outside kitchens. In my previous book, *The Path to Leadership*, I wrote about a young musician who never gave up hope of being promoted to the next level by his teacher. He practiced the same note tirelessly, continuously upskilling himself.

The boy joined a music class because singing was his passion. No matter how well he sang, the master never praised him and made him sing the same song repeatedly. While the other students progressed to more complex songs, he was stuck singing the same one. Three months passed, and he still didn't meet the master's expectations. Determined to improve, the boy decided that during the upcoming vacation, he would practice diligently so that by the time school resumed, he would be able to impress his master and be promoted to the next level.

On his way home for the holidays he dropped by an inn for refreshments where he saw a poster on the wall that read: 'Music Competition Tonight - The best singer will win an award of $500'. He decided to participate in the competition, choosing to sing the same song he had been practising for many weeks. Not only was his voice sonorous on the stage, but every note was strung together melodiously and harmoniously. He was awarded the first prize.

When receiving the award, he said in his gratitude speech: 'I owe this success to my music teacher, who made me practice this song to perfection. I worked extremely hard, never quitting or getting bored, even though I had to sing the same song repeatedly.'

A person who has learnt to be skilled develops a positive attitude, becomes passionate about their work, and ultimately progresses in life. Research has shown that inborn traits and skills are among the last to be fade, even when we become ill or when amnesia sets in. The Polish movie *Forgotten Love* (2023) is a perfect example of this. The film follows a surgeon suffering from amnesia due to a brain injury, who still demonstrates his surgical skills by helping those who are gravely ill and cannot access or afford a hospital.

We live in a fast-paced age driven by robots and artificial intelligence. The world is evolving rapidly the speed of which can be managed by maintaining a balanced pace between upskilling and upscaling.

When I first saw a driverless car moving around the streets of the San Francisco metropolitan area, I was amazed and apprehensive about stepping into one. Later, when I saw police robots at the Singapore Changi Airport, I was even more amazed and, somewhat bemused, watching a nearby officer casually sipping a cup of coffee. Many more such developments will likely be seen soon after this book is published. It can be concluded that this reflects the accelerating pace of upskilling and upscaling both of which stimulate the brain to work faster and more furiously.

Automation is beneficial as long as the human brain remains the driving force, introducing changes through halts and pauses to control dependency and addiction. Otherwise, humanity may feel the helplessness of not knowing what to do when the machine stops, a concept that E.M. Forster discusses in his essay 'The Machine Stops'. However, such a situation is unlikey to arise, as the current generation will always impart the knowledge of skills to the next, while warning them about the limitations of tools like artificial intelligence.

When a teacher learns to teach through interactive boards or electronic resources, it is a great example of upskilling. An example of upscaling, on the other hand, is when the same teacher is now branded as a global educator. Leaders must upskill themselves if they want to grow.

Effective Practices for Upskilling

1. Identify the area requiring upskilling. This depends on the demand for specific skills, which helps the individual advance. After identifying the need, assess the current skill level to pinpoint the areas that require improvement.
2. After identification, study the gaps and work towards closing them.
3. After closing the gap, the newly acquired skills can be further refined.

Example: The professor loves teaching history, despite holding only a post-graduate degree.

To improve their teaching, they need to identify a focal point of interest, for example ancient Indian culture, which aligns with their passion. Further, intense reading in the area will close the knowledge gap and strengthen the core understanding, ultimately leading to upskilling. In this case, upskilling would involve writing a research paper and acquiring a PhD.

Identification ⟶ Analysis of Gaps ⟶ Closing of Gaps ⟶ Further upskilling

It is, therefore, a step-by-step process. One who acquires many degrees solely for employability, without going through the process, cannot become versatile or truly skilled. However, consistent effort towards self-enhancement can bring the transformational change one desires. It is the evolution of the new and confident 'you'—one equipped with skills.

In today's world, we need to be inspired to keep growing.

> 'Live as if you were to die tomorrow. Learn as if you were to live forever.'
>
> —Mahatma Gandhi

For continuous growth and innovation, unlocking your potential is essential. Optimization requires a systematic approach, which includes the following steps:

1. Identifying your strengths and setting goals.
2. Evaluating your strengths and working towards accelerating them.
3. Accelerating your strengths and skills by acquiring ancillary professional skill sets.
4. Continuous practice through observation and analysis.
5. Embracing challenges and difficulties as stepping stones.

The end result of the above practices would be the development of emotional intelligence, leadership skills, and professional growth.

A few clear facts on the differences between upskilling and reskilling.

1. **Definition**

   Upskilling:

   - Refers to improving existing skills to stay relevant in the current role.
   - Focuses on a deepening expertise in a niche area.

   Reskilling:

   - Involves gaining a completely new set of abilities.

2. **Purpose or Aim**

   Upskilling:

   - Upskilling teaches adaptability.
   - Example: A digital marketer learning advanced techniques to stay updated.

   Reskilling:

   - Prepares individuals for a shift to new responsibilities
   - Example: A factory worker learning coding to transition into an IT-related role.

3. **Utility**

   Upskilling:

   - Used when aiming for career growth within the same field.
   - Useful when new technologies or methodologies are introduced.

   Reskilling:

   - Relevant when someone wants to change careers entirely.

Conclusion

The whole process of learning skills is like this:

> 'He who would learn to fly one day must first learn to walk and run and climb and dance; one cannot fly into flying.'
>
> —Friedrich Nietzsche

I met an interesting person at work one day. He could do anything, from painting to walking steadily while blindfolded. He could even play an instrument blindfolded. He was essentially a brain gymnast who trained himself with gym exercises to improve his cognitive abilities. The skill here is viewing the mind as an asset and training it to achieve the achievable.

Finally, what should be stronger than the skill is the will. A powered skill alone leads to empowerment.

Project

Divide your skills into two categories—technical and soft skills—and ideate. To develop technical skills, one must join coding classes, machine techniques, etc. To develop soft skills, communication and conversation-based activities are helpful.

A good relationship is not just about forgiving and forgetting, but about the transformative power of forgiveness. It can heal wounds, mend broken relationships, and bring about a sense of peace and harmony.

6

Learning to Forgive and Forget

Well, heaven forgive him! and forgive us all!
Some rise by sin, and some by virtue fall:
Some run from brakes of ice, and answer none:
And some are condemned for a fault alone.

—William Shakespeare

It is more of an adage when it comes to forgiving and forgetting. To learn to forgive and forget, one must first practice it. We can perhaps learn this best from young children who rarely hold grudges. Once, I saw two girls making sandcastles on the beach when a boy came running by and destroyed their castle. Naturally, the children fought and hit each other. The parents, who were sunbathing nearby, rushed in after hearing the commotion. The parents, trying to act as mediators, ended up arguing amongst themselves as they justified the actions of their own children. A lot of people joined in and started taking sides as the fight shifted from the main topic to personal insults. By sunset, a priest settled the quarrel and asked all to be religious. The three children had forgotten the fight that had taken place between them and had built a new sandcastle together. The priest reminded the parents to learn how to forgive and forget from their children's example.

Great nations have gone to war with one another, but history shows that wars do not define relationships forever. With time, perspectives shift, and reconciliation becomes possible. The fall of the Berlin Wall in 1989 symbolized such change—an end to division and the beginning of reunification, made possible through political will, social movements, and the determination to move forward.

I'm a firm believer that a sound mind resides in a sound body: *mens sana in corpore sano*.

If we are not emotionally strong, then we can never let go of past mistakes, which hang around our necks much like the dead albatross in Coleridge's 'The Rime of the Ancient Mariner', preventing us from attaining happiness and success.

How does one seek redemption from guilt and cultivate the art of self-forgiveness?

1. Write down what is bothering you and find the solution yourself.
2. Learn to treat yourself with kindness and remind yourself that the past can be forgotten, like a bad horror movie.
3. Learning to rebuild your identity after a personal calamity or tragedy can help in gradually overcoming even the most significant emotional consequences.
4. Learn from bad experiences, as they helps you avoid making further mistakes.

Story on learning from bad experiences:

No experience is completely bad; it is simply an experience to be remembered and learned from. The more you fail, the more you realize that nobody is born perfect. Holding grudges will never allow you to move on. We tend to hold grudges when we feel our trust has been betrayed, but in the long run, failing to let go of these grudges keeps us stuck in the past and prevents us from seeing the future. The only way to forgive and forget is by being empathetic, open-hearted, accepting, inventive, intuitive, open-minded, and understanding of the situation. Learning to let go is a challenge and a tremendously transformative process.

1. The day you acknowledge your emotions, you have accepted everything—including your failings and strengths, making you a 'better you'.
2. Empathy plays a crucial role in the process of forgiveness. It allows us to understand the other person's perspective, feelings, and reasons for their actions. This understanding can soften our hearts and make it easier to forgive.
3. Understanding the situation behind the offence can also help lighten the heart. This is different from empathy because situations can be short-lived and instantaneous.
4. The day I introspected and understood who I am, I was able to correct myself quickly by extending an olive branch to the person I was offended by. Focusing on your well-being and taking responsibility fosters greater humility and understanding.
5. The first thing students are taught in school today is the incredibly valuable quality of open-mindedness. This

quality not only fosters personal growth but also helps in believing in oneself and exploring new areas.

* * *

Once upon a time, two families lived in a small town. One was traditional and culture-bound, while the other was more broad-minded and open to newer ideas. One day, a traveller passed through the town and stopped at the inn for the evening. He claimed that he had an intricately designed box full of magical powers that could bring joy and unending happiness.

The traditional family dismissed this claim as a fallacy, believing that such ideas would distract them from the well-established beliefs they held. In contrast, the open-minded family was adventurous and eager to explore what was in the box.

When the box was opened, it turned out to be a piano. The traveler began to play beautiful melodies, filling the inn and the surrounding areas with sweet music. The traditional family drew closer and soon experienced absolute joy. The already broad-minded family, who were the first to approach the traveller, felt unending pleasure. The town became harmonious, and its people, grew into better individuals.

The lessons here were:

1. Open-mindedness bridges divides.
2. Opening our hearts fosters positivity.
3. Two individuals with opposing views can now work together.
4. A balance is struck between the old and the new, between tradition and exploration.

Forgiving and forgetting is an art that can be taught to young students as a virtue. Letting go of anger and embracing forgiveness is the path to harmony and progress.

The story of Rishi Durvasa and Maharishi Ambarisha, with the latter forgiving the angry saint Durvasa, illustrates the power of forgiveness in counteracting anger and fury, ultimately bringing inner peace and enlightenment. Buddhism is founded on being open, compassionate, and forgiving. In their book *Chicken Soup for the Soul*, Jack Canfield and Mark Victor Hansen highlight the power of forgiveness. Whether it's a major wrong or a minor blunder, forgiving someone is healing and allows you to move on with your life. You don't have to forget or condone what happened, but letting go of your anger improves your well-being and repairs relationships.

We all know that forgiveness offers numerous benefits, such as lowering blood pressure, reducing stress, improving anger management, and building stronger friendships. However, to me, it also keeps you youthful. In the end, who doesn't want to remain youthful? A youthful person brings joy to the people around them, and everybody seeks their company. The life force changes, and brings vibrant dynamism to life. As Daisaku Ikeda states, 'Ultimately, all human activities have as their goal the realization of happiness.' The Japanese way of forgiving and forgetting, well-known around the world, serves as a good example. It is expressed through the phrase *mizu ni nagasu*, which means 'let it flow in the water'. Through subtle expressions like softening a gaze and ceasing to harbour resentment, one lets go of anger and the desire for retribution. Remember the power of forgiveness, and the power required to forgive. Mahatma Gandhi, therefore, rightly stated, 'This weak can never forgive. Forgiveness is the attribute of the strong.'

The art of forgiveness lies in the four givings. They are:

Be generous
Be industrious
Be virtuous
Be empathetic

When one adheres to the above core values, one can understand why forgiveness is essential. The deeper the forgiveness, the stronger the values of generosity, hard work, embedded virtues, and empathy become.

By letting go of grudges, we open ourselves to healing and emotional freedom, which helps us thrive in both our personal and professional lives. The power of forgiveness is indeed great.

Forgiving doesn't mean forgetting the wrong or excusing bad behavior. Instead, it's a choice to release the hold past events have on us. When we forgive, we free ourselves from negative emotions that keep us stuck in the past. This allows us to progress with a lighter heart and clearer mind, focusing on growth, learning, and new opportunities.

Forgiving and forgetting isn't always easy, especially when the hurt is deep or the betrayal is severe. But once forgiveness is granted, it creates space for healing in relationships. It allows us to rebuild trust and strengthen connections.

In the end, forgiveness is an act of self-empowerment. It doesn't erase the wrong that was done, but it restores our peace and freedom.

Conclusion

Those who wish to progress know that the key is to forgive, forget all that is displeasing, and retain only what stimulates growth.

- Cultivate the art of forgiveness.
- Let the motto be peace over blame and retribution.
- Understand that it often comes with age.
- Acknowledge your feelings and accept every emotion.
- Let go of grudges; this is possible when you make a conscious decision.
- Finally, empathy lightens the heart and makes all problems of discontent and discord seem trivial.

Books to Read:

- *The Blind Side of the Heart* by Julia Franck
- *The Game of Opposites* by Norman Lebrecht
- *Ramayana* by C. Rajagopalachari
- *Prithviraj Raso* by Chand Bardai
- *Walking with Nanak* by Haroon Khalid

Imagine the satisfaction of being the first to find the ripest corn, knowing that you alone have the skill to reap a bountiful harvest. This is the feeling of accomplishment that early risers experience every day.

7

Learning to Be an Early Bird

'The early bird gets the worm' means that those who act first are more likely to enjoy th fruits of success.

Being an early bird has two connotations:

1. One who rises early and goes to bed early.
2. The quick, swift, and intelligent person who grabs the first opportunity that comes their way.

The chapter is devoted to the latter—be an early bird and gain from it. When walking through a mall in Delhi, I came across many posters advertising discounts for early birds. Tickets for various events also offered early bird discounts.

It is one way of taking advantage of buying products at a cheaper price. Early birds, therefore, reap significant benefits and earn great profits. In life, those who are punctual and plan ahead are sure to walk the path of success.

Among all the early birds, the lark is my favourite. Larks are happy, and the melodious sound of their song starts even before sunrise. Their sharp, tinkling notes often transition into a harmonious melody. The initial harsh buzzes and chips give way to beautiful music. The lesson here is to be an early riser— being proactive and planning ahead gives you time to relax and savour the rewards of your hard work.

The phrase 'early bird' holds different meanings for different groups of people:

1. For students, it signifies waking early to prepare for lessons, being punctual, and planning ahead. This way, when exams approach, there is less stress and a healthier, clearer mind to face them.
2. For teachers and workers, it represents seizing the opportunities that comes their way, giving ample time to assess the potential losses or gains and, make corrections.
3. To the marketing community, it is about early bumper sales, while for consumers, it symbolizes making a wise purchase.

The early bird, therefore, gets the best deal.

I am not an early riser, but has that made me less successful? While it is often said that early risers are successful, the reverse may not always be true. Early risers wake up with a fresh mind, ready to embrace the day with a sense of anticipation and excitement that only the rising sun can bring. I remember catching the first rays of the sun while on holiday in Darjeeling, from the guest room in our holiday home. It was such a magnificent sight that I couldn't help but write 'Happy Home'.

The lesson, therefore, is that with every rising sun, the best of poetry, music, and painting emanates. Here are some reasons why you should be an early bird:

1. Completing work on time by sticking to schedules and timelines.
2. Observing the environment around you to savour the best moments.
3. Starting your creative pursuits, such as music, writing, or painting, to get the best results.
4. Be cautious and alert enough to differentiate the chaff from the wheat, the good from the bad, and the daylight helps differentiate.
5. Finally, it helps all your senses, along with the mind and soul, to grow holistically.

Coming to the non-philosophical aspect of being an early bird, for me, it aligns with the routine of early learning. I am a quick learner and believe that being an early bird delivers the best results. In this case, the early bird learns quickly, as embracing change becomes easier without any delays.

The advantages of such early learners are numerous:

- They can accept new technologies.
- They always have a good backup plan.
- They are flexible.
- They have more time on hand to be innovative.
- They are the best team players.
- They can handle high-pressure jobs without feeling stressed, since they are not pressed for time.

No wonder one of the most popular proverbs is 'better sooner than later'. Today, it is cheaper to start a business than it will be tomorrow. It is evident that any venture taken up late in business often does not earn rich dividends, so it is right to state: be an early bird, lest you miss all opportunities.

Many animals are 'early birds', starting their day at dawn or even before. These creatures have evolved to take advantage of the early hours, whether for feeding, hunting, or avoiding predators. Here are some examples of early risers from whom we can learn valuable lessons:

- Among the first birds to rise are sparrows and robins, which are frequently heard singing during the 'dawn chorus'. To protect their territory and hunt for food, like worms, insects, and seeds, they get up early. Because there is less competition for food and the morning temperatures are milder, many birds take advantage of this time.
- Deer are crepuscular, meaning that they are most active at dawn and dusk. They evade daytime predators by grazing and drinking water in the early morning hours. The likelihood of encountering wolves or other predators is reduced when grazing at dawn.
- We like squirrels, but very few know that at dawn, squirrels are highly active in gathering food, seeds, and nuts to preserve for the day or winter. They acquire food in the early morning hours, before hawks and other larger predators become active.
- Frogs are only audible during the monsoon season when lakes and ponds are full. Certain frogs, such as bullfrogs, croak early in the morning to mark their territory or attract

mates. Their calls are amplified by the early morning silence, which facilitates communication.

Lastly, we must remember that the hallmark of early preparation and execution is what makes a person strong and energetic.

In addition to rising early, certain birds exhibit behaviours that require careful preparation, coordination, and execution in order to survive and flourish.

Crows are a prime example. They are renowned for their high level of intelligence and ability to solve complex problems. By hiding food (caching) in several places to recover later, they prepare ahead of time. They also learn survival skills by watching other birds and even people.

The activities of these birds and creatures drive home the point that rising early can help improve mental health, enhance productivity and offer several physical health benefits. Many people today, due to an overdependence on technology, suffer from insomnia and lack of sleep. The cure for this could be to wake up early in order to to handle challenges with greater ease. Moreover, good planning always gives you time for better decisions and allows you to stay focused on long-term objectives. Developing a habit of just waking up early is a choice, but it cannot be denied that this choice leads to fruitful results and success. The morning glory sets the mood for the right work and cultivates the right attitude.

Conclusion

An early bird rises, shines, and rests in its nest, dreaming of a thousand stars and the possibilities of the next day. If you are not an early bird, you might miss the bus. In life, we often realize our mistakes long after the opportunity has passed. Having a mentor to help you align with early rising is important. Mentors guide us in making the most of available opportunities by helping us set small goals and fulfill them on time.

- Consistency is key—step-by-step, small, consistent changes are more effective than drastic overhauls.
- Sleep well and create quality.
- Establish a wind-down routine—an hour or two before bed, with dim lighting and calming music to help you relax.
- Make life enjoyable by pampering yourself, such as making your own breakfast.
- Be patient and persistent—this is the core principle of routine life. Follow a schedule and make it a habit.
- It takes time, but celebrate small wins along the way.

Activity

Set aside a day to experience the rising sun, observe the companions around you—who need not necessarily be humans—and explore their paths to success and empowerment.

Commitment and responsibility are
the champions of all mantras to success.

8

Learning to Walk Your Path

I vividly recall the moment when my son, just eleven months old, took his first steps. We were in Allahabad at the time. His hands didn't reach out for support; he didn't look for guidance but simply thought and acted. To me, this was the beginning of him walking his own path—a journey towards self-fulfillment.

What exactly does it mean to walk your own path? It means selecting your route consciously. It also involved being attuned to your inner self and making decisions with purpose. Stepping into somone else's shoes may help you emulate them, but when you step into your own new shoes, you will know precisely where they pinch as you travel down your path. You have to be a risk-taker to walk your path. One can draw inspiration from the lives of numerous great professionals like scientists, doctors, or teachers, many of whom did not come from families in the same profession.

We have many examples of people who have decisively recognized their strengths and taken roads never before explored by their families. One such example is Dr A.P.J. Abdul Kalam. Even though his parents were not scientists, they were his role models who constantly ignited his mind with strong values. His exploration is exquisite and original. While we draw inspiration from mentors and successful people, but it is essential that we evolve and learn to choose a path that is best suited for us. We must identify our strengths and progress accordingly in order to assess whether we have chosen the right path.

As stated in my previous book, *The Path to Leadership*, we learn how to identify our inherent strengths that often lie dormant. Igniting these strengths helps us achieve our goals, something that requires commitment and dedication.

I once asked some of my students what they would like to become when they grew up. These were young students in grade five, each with varied ambitions and perceptions of different professions. Yet, they all shared a desire and dream to become something. The few who did not bother to think about the future were those felt secure in the knowledge their parents would decide for them. There was one boy who wanted to become a policeman. We wondered why the others looked down on such a profession and failed to recognize the respect that comes with the uniform. This student was someone who could naturally command the respect of his peers. These young children, unaware of the sanctity of uniforms, could benefit from understanding how different uniforms represent identity, responsibility, and the challenges the wearer must face.

What lessons do we learn while walking our own path? They can be classified as experiential learning, discovering one's uniqueness, and, above all, nurturing creativity. Each experience is a lesson, and learning from them helps you grow wiser and more knowledgeable.

How do I make my own path in life?

You simply have to follow four golden rules: goals, vision, purpose, and action.

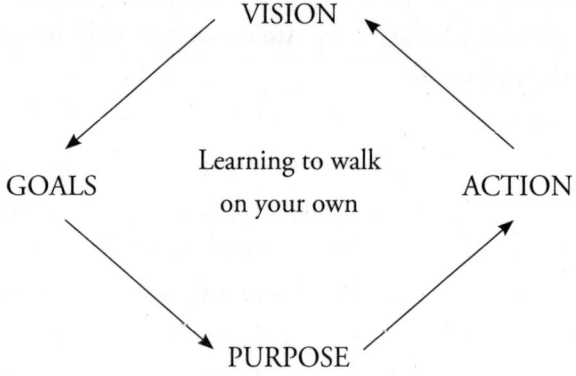

Vision: to dream and imagine a future state—whether for an organization or for oneself—and to make plans to achieve it. It is a well-defined picture in the mind of what one hopes to accomplish.

Goals: help us set priorities and keep us focused.

Purpose: gives meaning to our goals and makes them truly significant.

Action: power, passion, and play come together to bring about the actualization and realization of the vision.

When you walk your own path, you become more accountable for your actions. You begin to find solutions to your problems, and instead of being reactive, you become proactive. What do responsible people do? They don't play the blame game and pass on their failures to others. They ask for feedback and correct themselves. When walking on your path, accountability and responsibility rest on you. People often ask me if I have ever failed as a leader. I tell them, yes, I have made mistakes, and they called for greater responsibility in the workplace.

Taking responsibility is important, but don't you feel like people are pulling the rug from under your feet? The real question is: why didn't I notice when the rug was being pulled? There will always be people who will try to undermine you, and as a leader, it was my responsibility to be cautious, checking balances and taking my duties seriously.

It is often said that a wise man is usually found alone, while a weak man is always found in the crowd. Walking alone and facing the uncertainties of life makes you wiser because you find that you are stronger and more selfless.

The lion looks more majestic when it walks alone, not when it follows the pride.

An analysis of two kinds of people:

1. Children who have lost their parents at a young age and have had to grow up quickly with responsibilities. They represent those who walk alone—a great testament to their ability to stand tall and face life, irrespective of the obstacles in their path. They are mostly successful and loved by all in society.

2. There are those who have been raised in great abundance, and their lives have been so cushioned that they have received everything they asked for. They turn out to be selfish and seek companionship from similar-minded people. They give the impression of being born with a silver spoon. Only a few become their friends as they cannot be trusted.

Sweet are the songs of adversity, but the solo song is sweeter still. Haven't we seen a lone flower in a bush, standing tall and straight to face the sun? It draws its strength from the roots and soil from which it springs.

At the end of it all, walking your path alone teaches you the following:

ACCOUNTABILITY ⟶ RESPONSIBILITY ⟶
EMERGE STRONGER ⟶ MORE ADMIRED ⟶
FOREVER RELIED UPON

Very often, people ask me, when I fail in a particular project as a leader, 'Why could you not anticipate the factors that led to the disasters?' I often think of a quote by Barack Obama: 'If you're walking down the right path and you're willing to keep walking, eventually you'll make progress.'

On the spiritual side, according to Buddhist teachings, 'walking the path' refers to the journey towards nirvana. The mind stays focused and helps you progress.

The different connotations of walking your own path are:

1. You have to be true to yourself. When you put yourself first and walk your own path, you become more genuine and can become a leader, prophet and guiding light.

2. One can establish laws on self-discipline rather than following societal expectations or others' choices. The end goal should be the personal pursuit of self-good, which then extends to the good of others.

3. There is no competition in walking your own path. You are only in competition with yourself, so the path you choose is a space you enjoy, and the pace is solely dependent on you. The journey to your destination can be exhilarating.

4. When you walk your own path, you stay true to yourself and begin to believing in yourself. The day our learners conquer limiting beliefs will be the day they turn the impossible into possible.

5. When you walk your own path, you discover your potential, and no longer fear others imposing their thoughts on you. You become more cautious and less vulnerable.

See the boxes below and prioritise the benefits of designing your own trail.

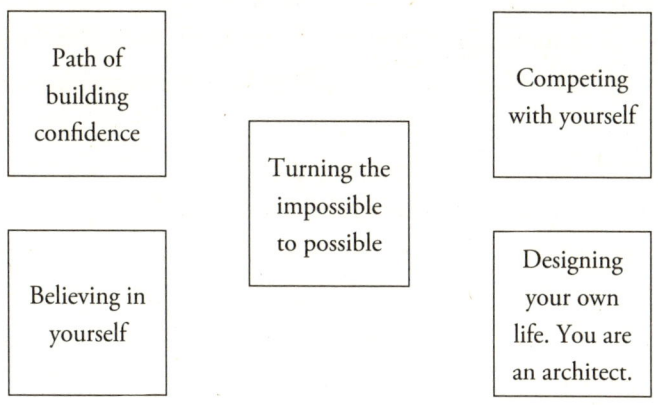

Path of building confidence

Turning the impossible to possible

Competing with yourself

Believing in yourself

Designing your own life. You are an architect.

Three wonderful realizations arise when you choose your own path and decide to walk it:

1. Self-reflection facilitates self-realization.
2. It encourages you to learn from your mistakes and allows curiosity to guide you in embracing the unknown.
3. Finally, it inspires you to keep track of your progress.

I have personally walked the hard path of switching jobs and, in the end, I was rewarded with a sense of gratitude and transformation that led to upward growth in my career.

It is about recognizing your calling and having the resilience to tread a new path. When we tread an unknown path, the exit becomes more rewarding. But the path is a lonely one.

> 'No one saves us but ourselves. No one can and no one may. We ourselves must walk the path.'
>
> —Gautama Buddha

Moreover, besides walking the path alone towards self-discovery and introspection, there are three areas that people often pursue individually: spiritual, educational, and business.

1. Walking your own spiritual path: Any path one takes is often driven by a desire to find eternal peace and happiness. For this, decisions must be resolute and firm. If Gautama Buddha had not walked his own path, he would not have reached the goal of enlightenment and self-realisation. Leaving behind his luxurious and comfortable life and

embarking upon a spiritual path led to enlightenment and he became known as 'the wise one'. Buddha devoted the rest of his life preaching *dharma* to all. Ashoka, the great warrior and might king, suddenly chose to walk his own path after the Kalinga war. His mind was revolutionised after witnessing the tragedies of war. He renounced violence and armed conquests and embraced *ahimsa*, which ushered in a new era of peace and prosperity.

2. Educational path: By designing effective teaching methodologies, a change is brought about in approaches to teaching and learning. This maximizes learning, and helps teachers become great mentors.

3. Business path: Most entrepreneurs often choose a path that only suits them. We picture a businessman in a formal suit, making countless plans filled with steps, goals, and objectives to achieve desirable results. Every entrepreneur walks on a defined path alone, one which relies on focus and concentration.

Walking your own path need not be lonely; it can be a powerful idea, leading to the creation of processes and, eventually, great results.

How to 'walk your own path':

1. Take up a project and try leading it with a few subordinates. It allows you to learn crucial skills like accountability, responsibility and tenacity.

2. Go for a stroll every evening and have a conversation with yourself—your thoughts and feelings. The path, indeed, becomes unique.

3. Turn your path into a trail. Try trekking and rock climbing—
   you will likely have to do it alone. But at the end of it all,
   there is a sense of achievement: I did it on my own.

4. Practice overcoming difficult circumstances with perseverance.
   Life's journey is not easy, and the path is often filled with
   challenges. However, it is through these challenges that
   we learn and grow. Walking your path means embracing
   the struggles. When obstacles arise, it is easy to feel
   discouraged, but it is important to remember that the
   most rewarding achievements often come after the hardest
   battles. Perseverance is the key to success. Every small step
   brings us closer to our goals. By facing challenges and not
   giving up, we grow stronger and learn important lessons
   that shape our future.

5. It is natural for people to seek approval from others.
   However, walking your path means being willing to make
   choices that align with your goals, even if they differ from
   the crowd. While advice from others can be helpful, it is
   essential to differentiate between helpful guidance and
   pressures to conform. Following someone else's path might
   seem easier, but it often leads to regret.

   When you walk your own path, you give yourself the
   freedom to choose the direction of your life. It's about
   recognizing that success has a personal definition, and only
   you can determine what it means to you. The journey will be
   different for everyone, and it is up to each person to define
   their own success based on their values, interests, and passions.

6. The power of persistence and focus. To walk your path
   and go far, focus is essential. It's easy to become distracted
   by the noise of the world and by the opinions of others.

However, real success comes from the ability to stay focused, no matter how long it takes to achieve your goals. Consistency, dedication, and hard work are the key ingredients for walking your path with purpose.

The journey is not always about the destination; it's about how we choose to walk along the way. By focusing on the present moment and maintaining clarity in our vision, we can navigate the ups and downs of life with ease. It is this dedication to your path that ultimately leads to the realization of your dreams.

Conclusion

'Walk your path and go far' is a reminder that true fulfilment in life comes when we embrace our uniqueness, and follow our inner compass. By walking our own path, we take ownership of our journey, grow in strength and wisdom, and ultimately reach our fullest potential. It is through our personal journey that we not only achieve success but also find peace. So, take that first step today, trust your instincts, and remember that the road may be long, but the rewards are worth it.

Learning never ceases. It is perennial and unending. A scribble in the notepad, 'What have I learnt today' is what needs to be retained.

—◦✕◦—

Curiosity is the first step on the path to meaningful learning.

9

Learn to Be Curious

The mind that opens to a new idea never returns to its original size.

—Albert Einstein

First, let us understand the adage 'curiosity killed the cat'. It is well-known proverb that warns people not to be overly curious or investigate things that could be dangerous or harmful. While curiosity is often seen as a positive trait, encouraging learning and exploration, this saying warns us of the potential risks of excessive inquisitiveness, especially when it involves delving into matters that are best left alone.

The Role of Curiosity

Curiosity is a natural human instinct. It is the key factor behind scientific breakthroughs, technological progress, and personal development. From childhood, we are taught to ask questions, explore the world around us, and seek answers to the unknown. Curiosity fosters creativity, learning, and innovation, and it is essential for the progress of individuals and societies.

However, curiosity can also have its drawbacks. When curiosity leads people to explore things that they don't fully understand or when it pushes them into potentially dangerous or harmful situations, it can cause problems. The phrase 'curiosity killed the cat' suggests that just like a cat, which might innocently explore risky places, humans too may sometimes put themselves in danger by being curious.

The Meaning Behind the Proverb

The proverb originated from the idea that cats, known for their playful and curious nature, sometimes explore spaces or objects that can harm them. For instance, a cat might be tempted to investigate a place that appears mysterious, such as an open drawer, a hole in the wall, or even a dangerous object, like a heated stove. The phrase implies that this curiosity could lead the cat to misfortune.

In a broader context, the proverb is a metaphor for human behaviour. It serves as a reminder that while curiosity is important, there are certain boundaries that should not be crossed. Some things in life are better left alone, either out of respect, for safety, or because the risks are greater than the rewards.

Curiosity can be of two types:

1. Good curiosity
2. Bad curiosity

Good curiosity generates good questions, demonstrates real concern and an interest in further research. It also nurtures attentiveness and leads to better analysis.

Bad curiosity, on the other hand, fosters negative traits like meddling, eavesdropping, and rubbernecking.

After all, don't we all know if it had not been for a scientist's childhood curiosity—watching the lid rattle over a pot of boiling water and wondering how movement is possible through steam—he might have never have conceived the steam engine? In a similar manner, had it not been for Archimedes' curiosity, he never would have discovered the principle of buoyancy and jumped out of the bathtub, shouting, 'Eureka!'

CURIOSITY → CRITICAL THINKING → ANALYSIS
→ GOOD FINDINGS → POSITIVE IMPACT

Learning to be curious leads to significant discoveries, and we should all embrace this.

Curiosity begins in childhood, and if it is not encouraged or answered appropriately, it can stifle the art of questioning, hinder learning and suppress further exploration. Therefore, it is essential that curiosity takes precedence in the classroom. Parents also must spend time with their children to foster experiential learning and nurture curious minds.

Curiosity is a powerful force that leads to deep understanding and innovation. I once knew a little girl who was so curious about the world around her that one evening, while relaxing in her grandmother's garden in a rural town, she happened upon a green-coloured stone. Curiosity got the better of her, and she kept it as a lucky charm. When she cleaned it, the little girl found a hieroglyphic-like script with a little picture on it. She took it to her history teacher, who knew an archaeologist. Lo and behold, the ancient script was decoded. The little girl's curiosity led to a discovery, illustrating how the world advances. This story is a testament to the fact that curiosity is not just a trait, but a driving force behind discovery and progress.

I have always loved the quote of Stephen Hawking, who said, 'Remember to look up at the stars and not down at your feet. Try to make sense of what you see and wonder about what makes the universe exist. Be curious. And however difficult life may seem, there is always something you can do and succeed at.'

Once, while travelling, I saw a little boy at an airport gift shop asking his mother several questions while she was selecting a gift for her friend. He kept asking her about the uniquely designed artefacts that were placed neatly in display cases and finally asked what the purpose of the shop was. A renowned professor standing in the queue to pay his bills looked at the young boy and said, 'Young lad, the shop is a souvenir shop.'

'Where from? How is it made? What's it used for? Why was it used? When did it exist?' These questions summarises all the W's and H—where, what, why, when and how—that further fuel the curiosity of a young mind.

Curiosity can be good, bad, as well as ugly. It needs be balanced and used with caution.

The Balance Between Curiosity and Caution

The key takeaway from the saying is that curiosity should be balanced with caution. It is important to ask questions and seek knowledge, but one must also recognize when further investigation might cause harm or have little practical value. There are situations where it is wiser to let things remain a mystery and trust that certain things are better left undiscovered.

For example, in today's digital age, curiosity about other people's personal lives can lead to an invasion of privacy. In relationships, being overly curious about a partner's past or secrets can create tension and damage trust. Similarly, curiosity about certain online content, such as dark web activities or dangerous challenges, can lead to unwanted consequences.

Good curiosity is a powerful tool for enhancing skills and fostering innovation, ideation, and invention, for both the individual and society. The end result is not just gratifying, but also positively impactful.

What is Curiosity and Safety in the Modern World?

In today's world, unchecked curiosity can lead to even more serious consequences. With the internet, social media, and easy access to information, people are often tempted to explore harmful topics or take unnecessary risks. The saying 'curiosity killed the cat' reminds us to be cautious and avoid the dangers of over-exploring.

While curiosity about the world, people, and knowledge can enrich our lives, it's crucial to know where to draw the line. Not all mysteries need to be solved, and sometimes avoiding certain paths can save us unnecessary trouble or harm.

'Curiosity killed the cat' serves as a valuable lesson on the importance of moderation. Curiosity, when kept in check and guided by wisdom, is a valuable tool for learning and personal growth. However, if left uncontrolled, it can lead to risks and harmful consequences. The proverb reminds us that while it is essential to explore and learn, there are moments when it is wise to step back, exercise caution, and resist the temptation to dig too deep. In the end, knowing when to stop is just as important as knowing when to ask.

Bad curiosity can lead to an addiction to information, resulting in a loss of attention and focus on what is truly important. This results in a cluttered mind filled with undesired distractions. It can also foster rigid thinking, reinforcing the belief that 'it is so'. This could lead to a closed mind dominated by a single perspective.

So, choose wisely.

How does one develop this?

By researching, evaluating, interpreting, debating, and then assimilating.

Curiosity Leads to Invention

A notable example is the famous scientist Dr Jagdish Chandra Bose. He said, 'What happens if you take a rich magistrate's son and educate him in a village school sitting beside the sons of servants and fishermen? He'll hear tales of birds and animals that make him curious about nature. And that makes him one of India's first scientists.'

Upon observation, Dr Bose discovered that plants also have life as they grow to become trees, and that a shared life process exists in both plants and animals. To support his research, he developed the crescograph, a highly sensitive instrument capable of registering even the slightest movements in plants.

These movements produced striking results, such as the quick quivering of plants in response to stimuli. This helped Dr Bose discover the parallels between animal and plant tissues, and proved that plants are living beings.

Further research and studies led to the discovery of plant physiology. Through observation, experimentation, and evaluation, it was proven that plants respond to various stimuli, revealing similarities between plant tissues and animal tissues.

Curiosity led to the invention of the crescograph. This instrument is used to measure the growth of plants. It uses a smart glass plate and a series of clockwork gears.

* * *

I once read the story of a young boy who loved butterflies for their wonderful colours. In fact, he would spend hours watching these beautiful, fluttering insects. He knew how every butterfly struggles to transform from an ugly caterpillar into a majestic creature. However, he had never witnessed this transformation himself.

One day, he came across a cocoon with a tiny opening, indicating that the butterfly was trying to emerge. He sat there for over ten hours, watching the butterfly struggle to break free from its cocoon.

Finally, sensing that the butterfly needed help, he took out a pair of scissors from his bag and cut a larger opening in the cocoon to pull the butterfly out.

However, what emerged was not a beautiful large butterfly, but a tiny creature with a swollen body and shriveled wings.

He waited for it to fly. Unfortunately, the wings neither expanded, nor did the swollen body shrink.

Unable to fly, the butterfly went on to crawl through life with shriveled wings. Here, curiosity killed the cat.

A friend once told me about a boy who asked too many questions about how a car has the power to run on the road. To satisfy this curiosity, his mother asked him to sit beside her and observe as she drove.

Each day, he learnt something new about the gears, the clutch, or the brakes, which only fueled his curiosity about speed and acceleration.

Each day after the ride, his mother asked him about what had he learnt. He always had a lot to say, but she never gave him all the answers. Instead, she encouraged him to satisfy his curiosity through observation, analysis and interpretation. He studied the theory diligently, feeling confident that he could drive the car even before reaching the legal age for a license. However, his mother never allowed him near the steering wheel, nor did she ever leave the car keys within his reach. His observations, learning, and analysis continued and his interest in mechanics and physics became apparent. His curiosity enhanced his learning, and he waited for the right time to get his license. When he turned eighteen, he woke up on the morning of his birthday to find a new car parked in the driveway. He asked her why she had not told him earlier to which his mother replied, 'You need to be rewarded, son. I could have purchased a new car long ago but, I have witnessed your passion, and wanted to reward you for being patient and waiting to drive until you got your license. I applaud you for using your curiosity to think critically and learn about mechanics and driving.' Sure enough, he went on to become an excellent sports car driver. My learning from this story is that curiosity helps enhance knowledge, which transforms into an ambition to know more.

One must play excellent games to spark curiosity, for only then can one can think outside the box.

What are the learnings from curiosity? They can be summarized as follows:

1. Anything uncertain can trigger a response that helps resolving issues and finding solution to problems. This process teaches you how to be a problem-solver.

2. When one is entirely focused on wondering and researching how the moon glows, the curiosity about astronomy can lead to becoming an astronomer. You become a researcher with a concrete conclusions.

3. All curious people tend to become thought leaders, as curiosity fuels critical thinking, which helps make thoughts more concise and precise.

4. Curiosity helps you recognize your analytical skills and strengths.

5. Curiosity keeps you energized, continuously pushing you to improve. It sustains a strong desire for knowledge.

6. Every student, young or old, retains lessons better when curiosity is nurtured. Even an average child could learn more effectively when curiosity is developed into understanding. Encouraging a child's curiosity by answering their questions yields good benefits by enhancing their learning.

7. Exploration satisfies curiosity. The emotions it generates are happier and more positive.

8. Curiosity keeps enthusiasm alive, but enthusiasm alone may not be enough to keep the mind open. One may be an enthusiastic worker, but when that enthusiasm is paired with critical thinking, curiosity becomes a powerful force for growth.

In the end, I would say that curiosity, while leading to discovery and solutions, does not necessarily close the case. In fact, it provides food for further thought, igniting the spark to think more and grow more.

1. **We can evoke curiosity and practice it through the following activities:**
   - How to Play:
     - Go on a group walk in an unfamiliar place, such as a park or museum.
     - Set challenges like spotting a specific type of plant, finding an unusual object, or uncovering a piece of history.
   - How It Sparks Curiosity:
     Promotes exploration and discovery while fostering observational and research skills.

2. **Story Cubes**
   - How to Play:
     - Roll dice with pictures on each face and use the images to create a story.
     - Each player can add to the story by interpreting the dice in their turn.

- How It Sparks Curiosity:
  Stimulates imagination, creativity, and curiosity about how different elements connect to form a narrative.

3. **Curiosity Jar**
   - How to Play:
     o Fill a jar with thought-provoking questions or challenges like:
       ▪ 'What's a skill you've always wanted to learn and why?'
       ▪ 'If you could travel anywhere, where would you go and what would you explore?'
     o Players take turns drawing a question and discussing their answers.

How It Sparks Curiosity:
Encourages reflection and curiosity about personal goals, interests, and the world.

Therefore, while confidence and answers can take you far, it is curiosity and questions that help you achieve milestones.

Diplomacy is an art.

10

Learning the Art of Diplomacy

'I don't want to be artificial,' said a friend. 'I believe in being genuine and calling a spade a spade.' In other words, 'I don't want to be a diplomatic person—sugar-coated, using profound words that sound persuasive.'

Is that what diplomacy is? According to the dictionary, diplomacy refers to the act of managing relationships between different countries. It also refers to the skill of dealing with people without upsetting or offending them. To me, it is more about building positive relationships to progress in life and creating a better society.

The Importance of Diplomacy in the Modern World

In today's increasingly interconnected and globalized world, diplomacy plays an even more significant role. International conflicts, economic crises, climate change, and the rapid pace of technological advancement all require the thoughtful and strategic application of diplomatic skills. Without diplomacy, countries may resort to conflict, leading to devastating consequences for individuals, economies, and societies at large.

Diplomacy is essential for peace-building, whether it is through formal treaties, humanitarian aid, or peaceful negotiations. It is through diplomacy that nations can work together to address global challenges, such as climate change, terrorism, and pandemics, which do not respect national borders. It is also through diplomatic channels that countries can maintain open trade routes, safeguard human rights, and support international cooperation in scientific research.

Challenges in Diplomacy

While diplomacy is a powerful tool for peace, it is not without its challenges. One major difficulty is the ever-changing political landscape. Governments and leaders may change, altering the priorities and approaches to diplomacy. Additionally, the rise of nationalism and protectionism in some countries can create obstacles to international cooperation.

Another challenge is the rise of non-state actors, such as multinational corporations, international organizations, and terrorist groups, which can influence or disrupt diplomatic efforts. In the face of these challenges, diplomats must remain adaptable, innovative, and committed to the values of peace and cooperation.

The art of diplomacy is a complex skill that requires patience, understanding, and knowledge of the world. It's not just about making deals or agreements, but also about building relationships, seeing things from different viewpoints, and working together for the greater good. In today's world, diplomacy is one of the best ways to prevent conflicts, solve global problems, and maintain peace. As the world changes, diplomacy will become even more important in shaping how countries work together in the future.

Diplomacy, as a subject, can be classified into many categories, including civil, cultural or international diplomacy.

Integration refers to any relation that results in mutual collaboration and effective results between two or more human beings or countries; otherwise, it is considered diplomacy. Diplomacy helps build good relationships. It does not require the gift of gab or being a great public speaker delivering impromptu speeches to impress people. Diplomacy is the art of expressing one's thoughts in a way that is neither belligerent nor intended to harm anyone. How does actual learning of diplomacy happen? There are several ways of developing such skills, and they can be based on five golden principles.

1. A good relationship between people is established through active listening and understanding different perspectives.
2. Working and being a part of collaborative projects with diverse members of the community only broadens one's horizons.
3. Always debate, discuss and deliberate on topics that result in a positive conclusion.
4. Be open to feedback on your communication style and improve it.
5. Finally, critical thinking enables well-reasoned decision-making and helps solve problems effectively.

TACT

Tact is the ability or talent to address difficult situations without causing conflicts or confusion. Before discussing the topic further, I would like to clarify the differences between civil, cultural, and international diplomacy.

Civil Diplomacy

I like what John F. Kennedy said about civility in his inaugural address, delivered during the height of the Cold War:

> So let us begin with anew —remembering on both sides that civility is not a sign of weakness, and sincerity is always subject to proof. Let us never negotiate out of fear. But let us never fear to negotiate.
>
> Let both sides explore what problems unite us instead of belaboring those problems which divide us.

A civil person knows his 3Rs very well: respect, responsibility, and understanding relations and relationships.

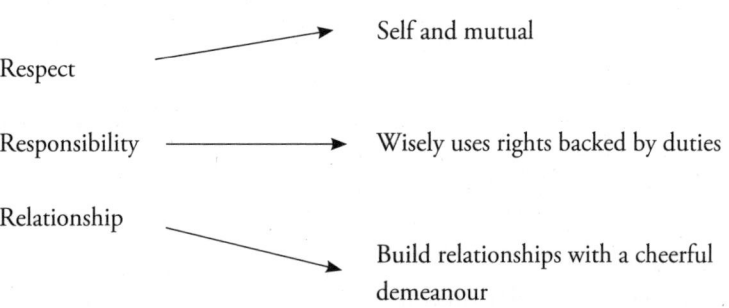

Respect   → Self and mutual

Responsibility   → Wisely uses rights backed by duties

Relationship

                                        Build relationships with a cheerful
                                        demeanour

Cultural Diplomacy

Cultural diplomacy involves the exchange of ideas, information, art, language, and other forms of culture between nations and people to foster good relationships and mutual understanding, especially in schools and other educational institutions. There should be a clear policy supporting school exchange programmes. This exchange need not be limited to foreign countries. A lot can be learnt from the various cultures within our own country. Culture should be the foundation of all applications and relations. I have seen students learning a lot through student exchange programmes, which can be organized at minimal cost even at a national level. Everybody appreciates diversity, but the challenge lies in encouraging it effectively. Today, cultural diplomacy as broken many barriers, creating a more connected world. It brings me great happiness and pride when I greet people outside India with folded hands and a 'namaste'. Similarly, I appreciate learning simple greetings in Spanish, German, or Japanese.

In the days of yore, ancient India witnessed rich cultural diplomacy between various kingdoms, to the extent that marriages between two different cultures were common practice.

Faxian, the famous Chinese traveller, came to India during the Gupta period on a pilgrimage to visit the Buddhist sites and to locate sacred Buddhist texts. He documented his experiences beautifully in his memoirs. He was impressed by the degree of religious integration in India, especially the coexistence and mutual respect between Buddhism and Hinduism, and returned home with valuable insights.

Another fine example is that of the great Mughal emperor Akbar. Akbar upheld strong values and was deeply committed to religious tolerance and cultural exchange. This allowed him to maintain cordial relations with other states and communities. Such cultural exchanges not only fostered peace but also contributed to the expansion of trade and commerce. Cultural diplomacy ensures the growth of personality and the development of open-mindedness among individuals.

International Diplomacy

International diplomacy is nothing but an effective foreign policy for each nation.

How does one develop diplomatic skills?

1. Be a risk taker. Challenge yourself to find solutions to difficult situations.
2. Communication in simple language is the hallmark of diplomacy, as it allows your purpose and intent to become clear. Often, people speak continuously and confidently but without knowledge—so not every confident person is necessarily right.
3. Understand situations calmly and serenely. A better understanding of the situation helps build bridges.
4. Develop the habit of practising good values and saying one positive sentence to yourself regularly.
5. Spend more time in the company of people with strong negation skills as all acts of diplomacy rely on effective negotiation for good business outcomes.

What is diplomacy between two people? It is nothing but good relations established through mutual respect and consideration. Trust and diplomacy are significantly compromised when faith and belief in one another begin to fail.

Do diplomatic people need to be modest, and vice versa? Let me explain the difference between modesty and diplomacy. A great deal of modesty is required in diplomacy, but diplomacy is not needed in modesty. Modest people, by nature, have this trait ingrained in them. Diplomacy, on the other hand, is a learned culture and must be cultivated.

Modesty vs Diplomacy

The most significant difference between modesty and diplomacy lies in the language each employs. Modesty is expressed through language that is kind, polite, and free of arrogance. Diplomacy requires carefully chosen words to convery ideas tactfully. Diplomacy plays a crucial role in resolving differences, facilitating prosperity, and ensuring peace and universal brotherhood.

Humour in Diplomacy

Humour is a wonderful asset that significantly supports diplomacy. Making people laugh before presenting the truth can help ease its acceptance. It can also create a more relaxed atmosphere, making it easier to find solutions to problems.

Many great leaders are renowned for their ability to effectively blend humour with diplomacy. For example, Herb Kelleher, the co-founder of Southwest Airlines, was known for skillfully resolving disputes with other airlines. He was often praised for his intelligence and wit.

When the Tata Nano, an affordable car designed for lower-income consumers, was first introduced, concerns were raised about its safety. Ratan Tata told the reporters, 'It's not meant to be a tank; it's a people's car.' This humorous remark effectively addressed safety concerns while emphasizing the car's intended purpose.

Learning the Art of Diplomacy

How do you respond to a compliment? If you're modest, you might say, 'Merci. I'm glad you liked it', or, 'I appreciate you saying that', or even, 'That's very kind of you.' An even better response is to acknowledge the person by name. Such modesty often builds stronger, more genuine relationships than diplomacy alone can. The recipe for modesty includes a welcoming tone, appropriate intonation, steady eye contact, and a genuine reflection of happiness and gratitude with a Buddha-like smile.

However, one shouldn't underestimate the importance of diplomacy. Chanakya famously said, 'Diplomacy is the art of building bridges, not walls.' Diplomacy is the art of understanding.

Tips on the types of phrases used in the most diplomatic sentences:

- Instead of saying 'not sensitive', it's better to say 'insensitive'.
- Avoid saying: 'You are not working hard; therefore, we are not progressing.' A more diplomatic way to say this would

be: 'If we do not meet this deadline, we may have to put in more effort or face some consequences.'

- Using phrases like 'would' is more palatable than harsh words like 'that is'. For example: 'We would be honoured by your presence tomorrow' sounds less direct than 'We expect you to be present tomorrow'.

- Disagreements can be softened yet remain clear by using specific words and phrases like 'actually', 'to put it bluntly' or 'to be honest'.

- Sometimes, we unintentionally sound rude by speaking too directly. For example, if someone suggests, 'Let's drive the car and park near the airport', replying immediately with, 'This is not a good idea, we should just take the metro,' can come across as harsh. Instead, it's better to offer a positive alternative without outrightly rejecting the idea. A more diplomatic response would be, 'Taking the metro will help us save time and avoid the stress of finding a parking space.'

My final take on what diplomacy means is that, in any language, one must adhere to *maryada*, which means dignity. When people talk with dignity and respect social norms, it fosters cohesion and unity in society.

'Diplomacy in leadership is winning the war on behalf of both the sides.'

—Lazarus Takawira

Albert Einstein was indeed humble when he spoke about the contributions of the Indian community: 'We owe a lot to the Indians, who taught us how to count, without which no worthwhile scientific discovery could have been made.' When our late former President of India, Dr Sarvepalli Radhakrishnan, served as the Indian Ambassador to the Soviet Union (1949-52), his diplomatic skills and intelligence played a pivotal role in establishing a good relationship between the countries despite their differing ideologies. He was a true diplomat who mastered the art of diplomacy.

A new kind of diplomacy has emerged, known as e-diplomacy. As it has become convenient to work online, e-diplomacy is also an art to be mastered. Since e-diplomacy involves the use of various tools, including social media, care must be taken to ensure cyber-security and safety.

It doesn't simply mean manners and discipline; rather, it is the art of being original, concise, and mastering the skill of using technology correctly. *The Oxford Handbook of Digital Diplomacy* describes digital diplomacy as a form of change management in global politics. How one presents oneself on social media reflects their personality, and naturally, we all want to be seen as knowledgeable, smart and intelligent.

Inculcating and learning good cyber manners:

1. Respect others
2. Respect privacy
3. Be mindful of your words
4. Recognize the signs of harassment
5. Fellow netiquette

Good Leaders and Good Diplomacy

If a leader believes in the dictum that to be truthful, one must be with words, they are often perceived as unpleasant. To be truly diplomatic, one must understand the client's point of view. Chanakya, the greatest statesman and the prime minister of the Mauryas, gave a lot of importance to diplomacy and peace, which he regarded as the best method to arrive at a solution. His form of diplomacy was rooted in *Dharmashastra*, which emphasized that good diplomacy establishes peace, avoids war by maintaining neutrality, secures peaceful borders, and builds friendships. It stressed the importance of strategic thinking and the welfare of society for effective governance. In the modern era, good diplomacy involved negotiation and networking, which help one build genuine connections. Trust between leaders and their subjects is established through these interactions. Learning diplomacy is essential for anyone who wishes to be a successful leader, whether in the military, education or business.

Practice

1. Always remember that our online activities leave digital footprints, so we must be cautious about what we post. In the digital space, diplomacy and discipline are essential. Diplomacy helps ensure compliance, and only a good leader truly understands the value of it.
2. At the level of education institutions, students gain an understanding of diplomacy by participating in youth parliaments and policy-making clubs.

3. At the corporate level, constant in-house training in the art of public speaking helps build diplomacy.

4. At both university and school levels, Model United Nations should be conducted as they help students become good delegates and diplomats by teaching essential skills like deliberation, negotiation and resolution writing.

5. Great diplomatic leaders have always been sources of inspiration. After all, who doesn't aspire to be a good leader?

Books to Read

1. *Digital Diplomacy: Theory and Practice* by Corneliu Bjola and Marcus Holmes

2. *Manners in a Digital World: Living Well Online* by Daniel Post Senning

Discovering our true selves is the biggest adventure of our lives.

11

The Unique You

In a world that often pushes us to fit in, there's something special about being yourself. Each of us is a unique combination of experiences, perspectives and talents that make us who we are. The phrase 'the unique you' is not just about celebrating the surface-level qualities—it's about acknowledging the deeper layers that define our sense of self. Understanding and embracing your uniqueness allows you to contribute to the world in your own distinct way.

The Importance of Embracing Individuality

From the moment we are born, we are all inherently different. Even when we share similar characteristics, our personalities, desires, and dreams vary. These differences make us irreplaceable. Embracing individuality is crucial because it allows us to remain authentic in a world that often values conformity over creativity.

When we compare ourselves to others, it's easy to feel like we're not enough. Society, through media and popular culture, often imposes narrow standards of success and worth. However, it's essential to recognize that our worth is not determined by meeting these societal expectations. Instead, it is determined by the unique qualities that define us. Embracing your individuality means accepting yourself for who you truly are—without the need for validation from external sources.

The Power of Self-Discovery

Understanding what makes you unique begins with self-discovery. This process involves reflecting deeply on yourself—your values, passions, strengths, and even your weaknesses. Through this exploration you begin to understand what sets you apart from others. This knowledge empowers you to make decisions that align with your true self, whether in your career, relationships, or personal growth.

Self-discovery isn't a one-time event; it's a continuous journey. As we grow, we discover new things about ourselves. Our uniqueness is not only shaped by who we are now but by who we have the potential to become. By staying curious and open to new experiences, we allow ourselves the freedom to fully express who we are.

Impact of Uniqueness on the World Around You

When you embrace your unique qualities, you contribute to the world in a way only you can. The diversity of thought, talent, and perspective you bring to any situation enriches the collective experience. Think of artists who create new forms of expression, innovators who revolutionize technology, or leaders who inspire others with their authenticity. All of these people are celebrated not because they fit in, but because they dare to be different.

In every interaction, you also have the opportunity to make an impact. When you embrace who you truly are, you inspire others to do the same. This creates a ripple effect, encouraging others to express themselves and follow their own unique paths. Ultimately, the world becomes richer, more vibrant, and more compassionate when people honour their individuality.

Overcoming Challenges in Embracing Uniqueness

Embracing individuality is powerful, but the journey to self-acceptance is not always easy. External pressures, fear of judgment, and insecurities can create barriers. We live in a society where trends and norms often dictate what is considered "acceptable" or "successful." Breaking free from these expectations can be difficult, especially when it feels like stepping into the unknown.

However, overcoming these challenges requires self-compassion and patience. It's important to remember that no one has everything figured out and that making mistakes is part of the process. The more we accept our flaws and imperfections, the more we realize they are a part of what makes us unique. It is through these challenges that we grow, learn, and ultimately discover who we are meant to be.

'The unique you' is not just a collection of your talents, interests, or achievements—it is the essence of who you are. It is the culmination of your experiences, thoughts, and dreams. Embracing this uniqueness allows you to live authentically and contribute in ways only you can. In a world that often tries to mould us into something we're not, standing tall in your individuality is one of the most powerful acts of self-love and self-expression. Embrace your uniqueness, and the world will become a better place for it.

Uniqueness is born when exquisiteness is supported by talent, creativity, and intense inventiveness. We are unique because we are all individually different.

Once, a seventh-grade teacher asked a group of students what made them unique and invited them to write two sentences describing their unique behaviours.

Many of the students wrote about how they enjoyed pursuing hobbies. While thoughtful, most responses were quite general and did not reveal anything particularly unique. However, one child offered excellent insight into writing. He wrote that each day he recorded in his diary the good deeds he had done and the wrong actions he should not have taken. For a seventh-grade student, this level of introspection was astonishing, and that is what made him unique. I never saw the boy again, but I could only foresee success for him. For a while, I wondered, 'What if we, as adults, benchmarked ourselves the same way?' I am sure we would be kinder, more thoughtful, more likeable, and perhaps even more useful to our communities. There was another boy who shared that he could draw any types of shipping vessel with great accucracy especially, submarines. No wonder it was a unique idea, but what made me love the idea was the thought that it stood different from the rest—unique and very sensible. The reason was apparent:

it is always a situation that helps us become unique. In the first case, the boy who wrote in his diary said that his grandfather did something similar, but instead of writing about his own actions, his grandfather recorded the good and bad deeds of others. The boy, however, took a different path. He realized he could become his own role model instead of modeling himself after someone else. This is what made his approach to self-reflection unique. The second child, the artist, was just as remarkable. His father was a submariner, and was often away on long missions at sea. In his father's absence, the boy thought of him constantly and channeled his thoughts into imaginative and unique drawings of submarines.

Not all unique people need to be exceptional. Unique people do things differently, but extraordinary people do things to gain importance. One becomes more important with the elevation of status. For example, when a school teacher is promoted to the role of the principal or the head of the school, the role itself gains an unique importance.

I know why it is essential to learn to be unique. Unique people can be changemakers and catalysts in society. Great philosophers and politicians have brought about changes in society through their ideas—changes that stand the test of time. Socrates, the ancient Greek philosopher, was perhaps the first to introduce moral and ethical traditions of thought. Though his philosophy was controversial, it strongly influenced thinkers of antiquity and continues to resonate even today. His ideas are studied by both medieval and contemporary scholars, and played a significant role in shaping the intellectual landscape of the Italian Renaissance, particularly in the development of humanist thought. This proves that his unique thoughts made him a great philosopher. Ancient Indian philosopher and political statesman Chanakya, also known as Kautilya, laid down the foundations for effective leadership and governance. He urged rulers to be cautious while selecting their ministers. This uniqueness earned him his reputation as a great political statesman.

All unique people have a spark in them.

They are not only one of a kind, but often become great protagonists and great change makers. They are authentic as their ideas are their own. As a result, they are emphatic. They are creative and fear no one.

How does one develop uniqueness?

Refer to my earlier book, *The Path to Leadership*, to help identify the 'I' in you. Tell yourself: 'I can be different. I have the trait of being independent—the strength and the hope to ideate and grow.' This sense of growth slowly becomes a part of of who we are. Your uniqueness is a form of learning that can unite and inspire.

You can create your own unique password. Think about it- how much time do we spend crafting a strong, unique password so that no one can copy it? So, it's time, folks, to create your own unique identity password. Follow your goals by relying on your strengths.

1. Believe in yourself and trust that you can accomplish the good you want to do.
2. Surround yourself with both young and older individuals who inspire you to think further and be more open-minded.
3. Identifying your talent and skills, honing them to the best of your ability is essential.

4. You can be unique only if you observe and analyze the world around you, allowing you interpret and choose what is best for you.
5. Never stop to learning. Learning is ceaseless. As Seneca wisely said, 'As long as you live, keep learning how to live.'

Somebody asked me during a podcast what futuristic learning in school education would look like. I thought for a while and concluded that while we continue to emphasize the three Rs, we must also understand it has to be combined with three Cs. Today, with three additional Cs added, this creates a truly unique combination.

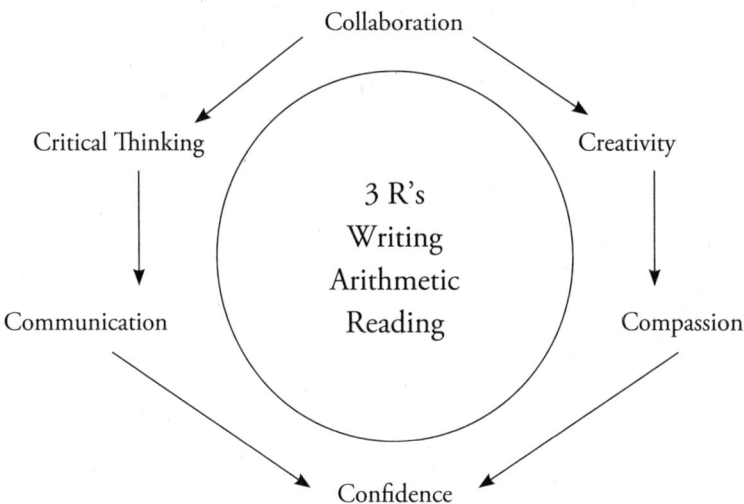

Uniqueness in Futuristic Learning with the three Rs combined now with six Cs for Greater Learning in school.

There are many essential ingredients in the recipe for creating a successful and lasting impact in education. Let us now understand how uniqueness can be fostered within companies that have fixed goals and structures. While structure is necessary, goals can be achieved in different ways. In fact, one can introduce innovative and unique approaches to a structured company without disrupting its foundation. For example, I know of a company where the employees enjoyed their work, even though the salary increments was not as high as in other companies. The perks were an investment in good health and a positive work environment. To encourage collaboration and gather diverse opinions, employees were given the freedom to express, innovate, and ideate. The following measures proved to be very attractive: 1) having an open project time, and 2) having a short coffee conversation before leaving for the day.

These practices spoke volumes about caring and delivering results without stress. Uniqueness was evident when multicultural thoughts and multiple opinions are welcomed in the decision-making process, bringing in the best results. Uniqueness, therefore, automatically brings in the desired results.

What does one mean when when someone talks about designing their future? There was once a young boy who said that he loved to 'fashion his future'. It sounded trendy, and I assumed that it meant he wanted to be more stylish. After a moment's reflection, I realized he wasn't talking about fashion in a literal sense, instead he was talking about changing his lifestyle. Great saints and gurus redefined their futures and fashioned them according to their realizations. This gave them a new lifestyle, one that helps them attain their goals.

Design Your Own Future

In an MBA class comprising graduates from varied disciplines, the professor asked them to design their future. The class giggled, thinking their futures were already set through the MBA course. It was only a matter of honing their skills and strengths among fellow professionals. The teacher drew on the blackboard and wrote wishes and quotes as 'thoughts for the day'.

The doctor drew a stethoscope and a patient, while the lawyer drew a scale to symbolize justice.

The engineer made a bridge and a dam.

Finally, the artist simply drew a circle and splashed a lot of colour inside it.

The professor looked at the drawing and asked, 'How can your life be a cycle of circles? You have yet to move forward and see life.' The artist replied, 'Life can be designed by your thoughts and philosophy, not by your degree.'

The other professionals were overconfident and competitive, believing that what they had studied needed only to be upskilled. The artist knew he was a good match for the professional, but in his own way, he excelled in thought and vision and could see a way forward.

A positive surprise in adapting to a newer style brings out the 'Special You' within.

The motto should be:

Learn to design your life.
Learn to keep the learning curve in future.

This fosters uniqueness.

Unique people are those who set standards for themselves and distinguish themselves from others. Their uniqueness becomes a personal brand and style. More importantly, unique people emerge as leader and inspire new ideas.

Good practices for being unique:

- Come up with unique and original ideas.
- Read stories and autobiographies of people who, against all odds, have made it to the top of the success ladder. People such as Walt Disney, Dr L. H. Hiranandani, Dr A. P. J. Abdul Kalam, and Malala Yousafzai have earned their success in the face of challenges.

Mistakes are stepping stones to better planning.

12

Mistakes Are Great Teachers

Learning from Your Mistakes

There's a famous proverb: 'What's the use of crying over spilt milk?' as what's done cannot be undone. True, but that isn't the end. There is always a new beginning. If the sun sets today, it does not mean it will not rise tomorrow.

We all make mistakes, and shall continue to do so. However, the golden rule is never to make the same mistake twice. New learning take place when new mistakes occur. The world would be a utopia if mistakes were not made.

Nobody is perfect. We all make mistakes, and many times our plans go wrong. Leaving everything to destiny would be a way of shying away from our problems.

The great French general and statesman Napoleon Bonaparte made several mistakes that led to his downfall. However, the mistakes he made have proven to be great lessons for the future generations—such as the importance of being courageous, leading from the front, and being fearless. He, therefore, could win and succeed in many battles like the Battle of Austerlitz during the Third Coalition War, and major victories in Italy and Egypt. For every war fought and won, he took full responsibility. Future leaders have learned that success comes only when one knows how to build a team with patience, training, and delegation. Make every member of your team feel important so that when mistakes are made, there is collective accountability. Mistakes help bring a new change in you. King Ashoka was known as 'Ashoka the Great' not because he conquered Kalinga after a brutal war, but because of the revolution of the mind. His mistakes led to misery and sorrow through his battles. Ashoka's Rock Edict 13 details the aftermath of the Kalinga war and how Ashoka embraces *Dhamma*, the Buddhist teaching of right conduct, nonviolence and tolerance. His transformation is also noted by foreign travellers, such as the Tibetan monk Taranatha, as well as in the *Ashokavadana*, noting how the 'Chandashoka' ('Ashoka the fierce') transformed himself into 'Dhammashoka' ('Ashoka the righterous'), a lover of peace and equality.

Mistakes and Learnings

If we need to grow, we must learn from the mistakes we make. Mistakes are stepping stones to better planning and improvement, ultimately leading to success.

The process of learning and improvement starts when we establish the right mindset for progress. This happens when one follows four important steps. They are:

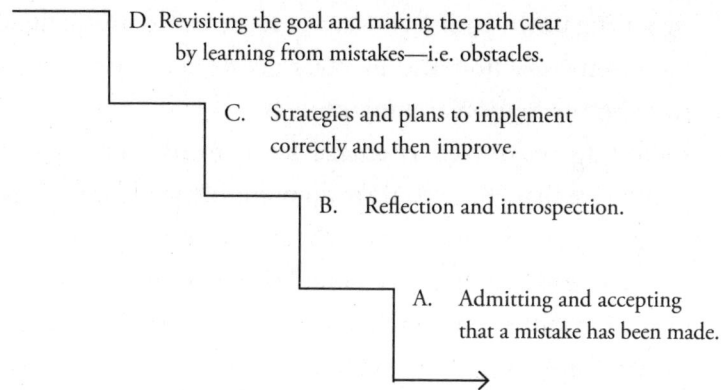

D. Revisiting the goal and making the path clear by learning from mistakes—i.e. obstacles.

C.   Strategies and plans to implement correctly and then improve.

B.   Reflection and introspection.

A.   Admitting and accepting that a mistake has been made.

A. Accepting Mistakes

It takes a lot of courage and humility to accept mistakes. If one finds it difficult to admit a mistake to someone they've wronged, try practicing in front of any dummy object first. This will help you learn how to confront the situation, and gradually, confidence will develop, allowing you to confront the person face-to-face. Not all film stars can be great orators or public speakers because many of them only participate in dubbing and speak in front of a camera, often delivering a limited number of dialogues one at a time. Courage and confidence are built when you speaks face- to-face.

First, accept that a mistake has been made by you. You must start by convincing and telling yourself that you have made a mistake. The next step is to admit the mistake if another party or entity is involved.

B. Reflection and Introspection of Mistakes

1. Introspection helps in examining and delving deep into issues and motives that have led to mistakes. It can be done

by jotting down your feelings, a practice called journalling. Good introspection also involves giving space to yourself through meditation and mindfulness.

2. Reflecting on oneself is crucial for personal enrichment, even more than growth. If we do not understand ourselves, we cannot understand anybody else. Every reflection on the self leads to improvement, which is why mistakes, once committed, are rarely repeated. Here is a wonderful story my friend told me of an overconfident potter: Once, Shyam, the potter, was asked to make a dozen clay vases for an exhibition hosting a charity sale. Shyam was in a great hurry, so he asked his apprentices to make them. Since they were being made specifically for a charity sale, with only a day to spare, the vases were hurriedly crafted and sent to the agency. The cartons of clay vases were returned after the sale, along with a note saying, 'None of them were enticing enough to be bought. They were oddly-shaped and did not look attractive.' The note further added that the management committee had canceled all further orders.

Shyam was upset and reflected upon his mistakes. His overconfidence, underestimation of a charity sale, and improper delegation of work were the reasons. However, he did not give up. Along with the rest of his team, we worked hard to correct the mistakes and sent new samples to the agency, emphasizing the personal touch involved in making the new vases. The following year, all his vases were sold, and Shyam received flattering compliments. Reflection taught him two great lessons:

i. Mistakes are opportunities to learn from, and one must not act hastily due to underlying overconfidence.

ii. Every mistake must be turned into a lesson; this alone strengthens both work and character.

iii. Reflection helps in identifying issues and the necessary corrections.

C. Strategies and Plans

Before any strategic planning, the vision, mission, and values must be spelt out and aligned with either personal or organizational goals. The goal path and plan should then be executed tactfully.

D. Revisiting the Goals

After introspection, reflection, and planning, the final step is to revisit your goals and remove any stumbling blocks. Breaking down goals helps in refashioning and redesigning projects, ensuring smooth progress. Not only does breaking down goals aid in managing them, but it also helps with time framing. Revisiting goals closes gaps and addresses loopholes, making mistakes feel like a thing of the past.

Mistakes may cause misery and unhappiness, but they are also lessons that empower us:

1. Mistakes provide valuable feedback, leading to self-assessment.
2. The unexpected insights we gain after making mistakes accelerate our innate potential, thus leading to great innovations.
3. One feels even more encouraged to work harder, and as a result, resilience becomes a core value.

Conclusion

King Alfred the Great firmly believed that mistakes are essential for acquiring wisdom. Had he not secured peace with the Vikings, a powerful enemy, he could not have gone ahead with his reforms in the reconstruction of Wessex and beyond.

On the contrary, Maharana Pratap, the Hindu Rajput ruler of Mewar, displayed great courage and bravery in the face of challenges. His humility, however, became his weakness. He faced the overwhelming Mughal army of Akbar with dauntless courage and perseverance.

He who makes no mistakes, makes nothing.

Create a pocketful of sermon. A reference guide for when mistakes are made:

1. Mistakes teach us valuable lessons: One of the most important things that mistakes teach us is what doesn't work. Every mistake carries with it a lesson about what went wrong, why it happened, and what can be done differently in the future. These lessons are not always easy to accept, but they are often the ones that stick with us the longest.

2. Mistakes build resilience and perseverance: Mistakes teach us to keep going, even when things don't go as planned.

3. Mistakes encourage creativity and innovation: The invention of the microwave oven was an accidental discovery when an engineer Percy Spencer noticed that a candy bar in his pocket had melted due to the radar equipment he was working with. These moments of serendipity remind us that mistakes can lead to breakthroughs that we would never have imagined otherwise.

4. Mistakes teach humility and self-reflection: When we make a mistake, it reminds us that we're not perfect and that there's always room to grow. This process of self-reflection helps us recognize our strengths and weaknesses. It allows us to grow emotionally and mentally, giving us a deeper understanding of who we are.

5. Mistakes are not something to fear or avoid: They are crucial for our growth and development.

I truly believe that making mistakes and developing humility is a thousand times better than gaining success and becoming arrogant.

—◁✕▷—

If thoughts are young and dynamic, the heart never wrinkles.

13

Keep Your Heart Young Forever

A heart that loves is always young. Daisaku Ikeda states, 'Youthfulness is not determined by age. It is determined by one's life force. One who possesses hope is forever young. One who continually advances is forever beautiful.'

We have a choice: do we want to be known as 'old and wise' or 'young and beautiful'? Both expressions, if combined, might be ideal. However, the evolutionary process of mankind speaks of inevitable physical and mental changes. We evolved from *Homo habilis* to *Homo erectus* to *Homo neanderthalensis* to, eventually, *Homo sapiens* traversing seven stages.

Whichever stage mankind goes through, ageing and well-being are always prime factors and concerns to keep in mind. Staying young forever is not possible, but remaining young at heart and soul is a personal choice. The 2007 documentary *Young@Heart* depicts that you are never too old to rock the world. The stereotypical age group barrier can be broken if the will and enthusiasm are there to pursue your hobbies. No doubt, what mainly contributes to a healthy heart is exercise, diet and good habits, but what nurtures a lively and young heart is the ability to practice. A good, young and lovely heart not only builds a positive exterior but also enriches a grateful and happy mindset, leading to an improved quality of life. The three beautiful mantras to a great quality of life are: Live, Love, and Laugh.

Live Life to the Fullest

Before learning how to live, we should be mindful that life is a journey, not a destination. Every moment, therefore, counts and every challenge must be embraced positively, as the lessons of life go back to our great beginnings. Setting boundaries, staying healthy, and being flexible help one live life beautifully. Being true to oneself and accepting life's challenges with grace enhances the health of the heart. Walking your own path (refer to Chapter 8) enables a smooth, independent, and more futuristic life filled with gratifying successes.

There is the story of a very beautiful woman who is ambitious and finds that each day, life is only a big rush— hectic and stressful. She could meet all the deadlines, but at the cost of sacrificing all her personal time. One day, while lying in bed, she realized that she needed bring cheer to her life by doing something very different. She went to her boss and asked for a day off, and the boss readily agreed. Remember, very few of us actually think the boss will ever let us take a day off, and so we never ask for it. The next day, she went to the mountains and took long walks into the woods, stopping to listen to the chirping of the insects and the birds. She then got herself a cup of coffee at a nearby café and observed all the young people enjoying themselves, feeling as if there were no tomorrow.

Life doesn't always need to be defined by achievement. Life is about finding joy, taking short trips, living in the present—one moment at a time.

Never wait for a perfect moment—simply having the courage to try new things is also a step towards life's success. Travel to an unknown place for a transformative experience, endless opportunities for adventure, and self-discovery. There is great joy in observing little things. A gratitude journal certainly helps in evaluating self-joy.

We have many fine examples of many great leaders who have shown how life can be lived to its fullest. Srinivasa Ramanujan, the famous mathematician, only had some numbers in his dreams, but once that became a passion, he lived by it. He was a very lonely person, but he found meaning in this loneliness. I knew how to live. Life is one great reminder of deep dedication to one's hobby against all odds, which can simply lead to amazing discoveries and equations. As for me, life has no meaning unless it expresses a thought of God.

Laughter

Learning to laugh is not everybody's cup of tea—it needs to be cultivated. It has been proven to be a powerful tool that empowers individuals with a strong heart, leading to a positive mindset.

In the yogic tradition, laughter aligns with truth, consciousness, and blessing. It is a rhythm that builds a sense of collective joy. This kind of laughter is known as exercised or intentional laughter. We can teach ourselves to laugh every day.

1. Start your day by looking into the mirror and smiling at yourself. While browsing through the newspaper, even an e-version, look for the cartoon section first, and then move on to read the more serious news articles.

2. Find humour in every situation and try breaking down large and complex problems into smaller parts. A bad day with your boss can be lightened by playfully imagining what might have caused their bad day, and laughing as you explore possible solutions. Be light-hearted, and laugh at mistakes. Always learn to laugh at yourself, which begins by conversing with yourself. A friend of mine once joked that when she looked at the wrinkles on her forehead, she suddenly thought of Albert Einstein, who inspired her to dream big.

   Whenever you laugh, remember to share it with others because laughing is contagious. Witty observations make life more amusing and turn everyday living into a joyful experience. Good leaders are humorous, witty, and intelligent, and they know how to use the techniques mentioned above to bring the team together.

   Watching cartoons can bring about a great sense of relaxation. Similarly, watching comedy channels can be equally entertaining and therapeutic. Laughter truly is the best medicine.

Three tips for embracing laughter are: develop a good sense of humour, know your humour, and like your humour.

Like What You Do

> 'Love the life you live. Live the life you love.'
>
> —Bob Marley

Whatever we do must have self-worth and self-respect. Without love in our actions, life becomes a meaningless drudgery.

Oscar Wilde's short story *The Selfish Giant* beautifully illustrates this. In the story, the giant had a garden where it was forever winter; the flowers never bloomed and the birds never chirped because the giant was selfish and never allowed children to play in his garden. However, the moment the children secretly entered and began playing, despite the restriction, the garden transformed. Flowers began to bloom, birds returned, and joy filled the space. The giant's heart blossomed with positive energy and growth.

We begin to enjoy our profession because we are passionate about it. Imagine you are forced to do something you dislike. A good cook prepares delicious food out of love. An average cook does it mechanically, while a bad cook ruins it entirely. The heart thrives on passion and fondness. Sometimes, we may need to develop a liking for something, and doing so helps us remain young and healthy.

Find joy in what you like to do. I know of a doctor who gave up his practice and went to the mountains to write a book on hiking. During one of his adventures, a comrade asked if he could ever shift his entire perspective on hiking and take up something completely new. The doctor replied that being a doctor was nothing more than a form of service or a profession to him; however, hiking, walking and talking to people was something he truly enjoyed. There is a profound difference between something you do for a reason and something you are deeply passionate about.

As teenagers, we were upset when our father was posted to a small, woeful town. But the moment we were in good company and surrounded by mother nature, we started to feel more energetic and positive each day. The initial disappointment and fear soon gave way to health and joy.

Explore, empathize, and embrace changes so that your heart remains young and healthy. At sixty, you can feel like a sixteen-year-old and lead a life of happiness and joy.

As we go through life, age comes to us all. Over time, our bodies change, our minds grow, and the world around us evolves. Yet, one of the most valuable gifts we can give ourselves is the ability to keep our hearts young forever. A youthful heart is not defined by age but by the way we approach life, the way we connect with others, and the joy we find in everyday moments. It's about fostering curiosity, compassion, and resilience while staying optimistic despite life's challenges.

Power of a Positive Attitude

One of the most important ways to keep your heart young is by staying positive. Life has its ups and downs, and it's easy to feel overwhelmed by challenges. But a youthful heart stays hopeful and strong during tough times. Rather than viewing obstacles as roadblocks, it sees them as chances to grow. A positive attitude helps us bounce back from setbacks, learn from our mistakes, and move forward with energy and determination.

Approaching life with optimism doesn't mean ignoring hardships or pretending that everything is perfect. Rather, it's about choosing to focus on the good, appreciating the small joys, and believing in the possibility of better days ahead. When we keep our hearts open to positivity, we not only uplift ourselves but also inspire others around us to do the same.

Stay Curious and Embrace New Experiences

Another important way to keep your heart young is by staying curious and open to new experiences. A youthful heart loves to learn, explore, and discover. Whether it's picking up a new hobby, visiting a new place, or reading about something unfamiliar, trying new things keeps your mind active and your spirit lively.

Curiosity encourages growth and keeps us from stagnating. It reminds us that we can always improve, no matter how old we get. It's the spark that drives innovation and creativity and keeps us feeling alive and excited about the world around us. By staying curious, we continue to learn, grow, and adapt, ensuring that our hearts stay youthful and full of life.

Nurture Relationships and Show Compassion

Keeping your heart young also means nurturing relationships that bring you joy and showing kindness to others. Connecting with people is a key part of staying youthful, as it allows us to share our lives and experience the world in meaningful ways. Friendships, family bonds, and even small, everyday interactions help keep our hearts warm and joyful. When we focus on positively impacting others, we not only enrich their hearts but also keep our own hearts open and young.

Take Care of Your Body and Mind

Though the heart is often seen as a symbol of emotional vitality, taking care of your physical health is also essential for keeping your heart young. Engaging in regular physical activity, eating nutritious foods, and getting enough rest—all of it contributes to maintaining a healthy heart and a youthful spirit. A healthy body enhances our energy levels, boosts our mood, and helps us face daily challenges with vigour.

Equally important is taking care of your mental well-being. Practices like mindfulness, meditation, or simply taking time for self-care help keep the mind clear, calm, and focused. When we tend to nurture both our physical and mental health, we create a solid foundation that allows our hearts to remain strong and youthful, regardless of our age.

Embrace Change and Let Go of Regret

Finally, keeping your heart young requires the ability to embrace change and let go of regret. As we age, we often reflect on the past with a sense of nostalgia, or even remorse, for things we wish we had done differently. However, holding onto regret can weigh heavily on the heart and prevent us from fully embracing the present.

A youthful heart is not anchored in the past but is open to the future. It understands that life is ever-changing and that every day is a new opportunity to grow, to learn, and to start fresh. By letting go of past regrets and embracing change, we free ourselves to live more fully and with a heart that is full of possibility.

Conclusion

What makes the heart young?

A teacher is always young at heart because she is always in the company of young minds, with whom they must align their thinking as well. I remember two drama teachers, both quite elderly at the time, talking amongst themselves. Both were around sixty-five years old, but since they were so good at their job, the institute decided to retain them on a consultancy basis. One day, a young parent of a five-year-old child, out of respect and curiosity, asked the two women about their age. With a light-hearted, carefree spirit, they replied, 'Hey, there's a traffic jam on our road of age. We're stuck as sixty and sixty-five, and we don't think we wish to move beyond that.' The young mother listened and told her friends that age is as much about the mind and heart as it is about numbers. After all, only a cardiac surgeon knows the shape, and the passport will confirm you real age, but in reality, keeping the heart young is all within us; feeling fit and positive.

At the end of it all, we can always lower the age of our heart by eating a healthy diet, following a good lifestyle, and maintaining a healthy weight. Always keep a child-like curiosity alive, and explore different paths. You will often find that the road less taken has actually been one that has led to greater and meaningful discoveries, culminating in immeasurable happiness and joy.

I tell myself growing old is inevitable but growing up is optional. Staying young is a skill—let the heart never wrinkle.

Define your own life.

14

Script Your Freedom

When I looked up at the sky one morning, I saw a flock of vultures flying effortlessly, literally gliding for a long period of time, flapping their wings and soaring into the open space. It seemed as though they were enjoying the kind of freedom everybody wants. These beacons of rebirth have their own code of conduct, which they follow even while enjoying freedom. In the same manner, freedom comes not only as a right but with responsibility and duty.

What is freedom?

Freedom is the right to act, speak or think as one wants. There are different types of freedom, although, the most important one is political freedom. During the era of imperialism, the domination of one country over the other curtailed the freedom of the natives belonging to the land. As a result, the countrymen, in order to enjoy that rights guaranteed by freedom, desired a free and independent country. The political leaders scripted the freedom of every citizen by drafting a constitution. Based on this, individuals enjoy certain rights such as freedom of religion, property, education, and many more that impact their lives. With so much available, it becomes imperative that one should know and learn how to script one's freedom.

Scripting Your Own Freedom

One has to understand what kind of freedom one wants. Most countries have attained independence, but true emancipation in certain parts of the society is yet to be realized. 'Script your freedom' is a powerful reminder that freedom isn't something that's handed to us; it's something we must claim, nurture, and protect. Whether it's personal, social, or digital, freedom is an ongoing process that takes effort and courage. By taking control of our stories, challenging societal limits, and actively shaping our paths, we can create a life that reflects our true selves. The script may not always be easy to write, but it is always ours to create.

True freedom is not about a smooth journey—it is about the courage to keep moving forward despite the challenges. Every obstacle overcome is a step closer to reclaiming one's autonomy and asserting the right to live by one's own script.

I recall an incident when, in a grade five class where the teacher asked the students to write about the kind of freedom they wanted most. Almost all of them wrote that they wanted to have the freedom to own a cell phone and use it like an adult. Upon reviewing their answers, the teacher discussed the idea of using technology with rules and duties. The students understood why it was not the right age for them to have unrestricted access to cell phones. One must learn how to build their own freedom. Many leaders exercise abundant freedom in their careers, but by the times they reach their mid-fifties, they burn out.

It is here that one must learn how to script their freedom. There are eight important steps to developing personal freedom, which is foundation for all other forms of freedom.

- Understand what is important and prioritize.
- Learn to always make yourself valuable by identifying your strengths and demonstrating them at work. Learn to internalize your thoughts and ideas first, and be your most original self.
- Learn to be accountable for all your decisions. You have to be accountable for life's problems, whether micro or macro.
- Failure is not to be accepted as a possibility. It is a roadblock to freedom, and you can remove it.
- To script freedom, there needs to be a goal. When goals are accomplished after overcoming various challenges, our skills improve and we can enjoy more freedom.
- Converse with yourself as you script your freedom.
- Ask yourself: 'What stops me from making decisions?', 'How can I build confidence in my decision-making?' Remember, you don't have to intelligent to make decisions-you need to wise and pragmatic, rather than just ambitious and practical.
- Finally, always keep happiness and gratitude at the core of your personal freedom. There is no path to freedom; freedom itself is a path, and so is happiness.

It is said that all good leaders know that a life of freedom rests upon the following pillars:

- Define your freedom first.
- Create a freedom model.
- Maintain strict discipline.
- Evaluate the expectations that are met.

What does freedom mean to me, and how exactly is freedom defined?

'Freedom is the freedom is to say that two plus two make four. If that is granted, all else follows.'

—George Orwell, *1984*

To me, freedom is the ability to do all that one pleases, without hurting others. It stems from breaking free the shackles of exploitation that encroach upon freedom. There are different kinds of freedom, and yet one may not experience all of them.

Overcoming Challenges in the Pursuit of Freedom

Scripting your freedom is empowering, but it comes with challenges. The journey to personal and societal liberation requires resilience, perseverance, and the courage to overcome obstacles. Fear of failure, societal judgement, and opposition from those who benefit from the current system are just a few of the barriers one may face.

The Role of Technology and Digital Freedom

To 'script your freedom' in the digital world means taking charge of your online presence and making sure your privacy is protected. This involves using tools like encryption to secure your data, supporting digital rights, and being careful about how your personal information is shared. It also means standing up against digital monopolies and advocating for a free and fair internet where the freedom of expression isn't censored or limited.

Social and Political

This aspect involves standing up against injustice, speaking out against discrimination, and using your voice and actions to create real change. The struggle for freedom, in this sense, becomes a collective effort—one that requires not only personal courage but also the support of others who share the same goals.

True Examples of the Definition of Freedom

The best example of freedom is knowing how to live in a state of free thinking and independent working, which can only happen if one takes into account mutual freedom and respect for each other. So, it is necessary that we define our own freedom and see that it doesn't interfere in anyone else's independence or become an obstacle to the social process. Once freedom is defined, the next step is to create a beautiful and sustainable freedom model.

A freedom model depends on four main pillars. But before we do that, we need to understand that a freedom model is designed for personal development, which ultimately enhances the development of the country or nation in which we live. We often take freedom as a right without knowing the responsibilities and duties that come with it. A beautiful freedom can be scripted if we base it on four main pillars: Firstly, we must define the purpose for which we seek freedom and develop a genuine passion for it. Secondly, we need to examine what kind of action must be taken to love the purpose and make it a reality. Once this process begins, it is essential to maintain a strong belief in ourselves and that freedom is attainable. Everybody is seen as an accelerator, a multiplier, and a beautiful partner in this journey. To attain freedom, one should have the courage of conviction and the ability to set the right goal before moving forward with the action. It is all based on goals, purpose, action, and belief, which together lead to the attainment of our desired result.

Discipline

What are discipline and freedom? They are deeply interrelated. Freedom means choosing what is good for oneself, while discipline is the inner awakening—the awareness that balances one's desires with one's needs. Without discipline, one cannot enjoy any kind of freedom. We need to understand what kind of discipline needs to be followed.

The pillars of discipline include: acceptance (embracing the odds), strong willpower (strength of mind), diligence, hard work, and persistence.

To successfully script your freedom, it must rest upon these pillars of discipline.

Discipline is brought about by adopting good habits and practising them in order to succeed in life. Discipline can

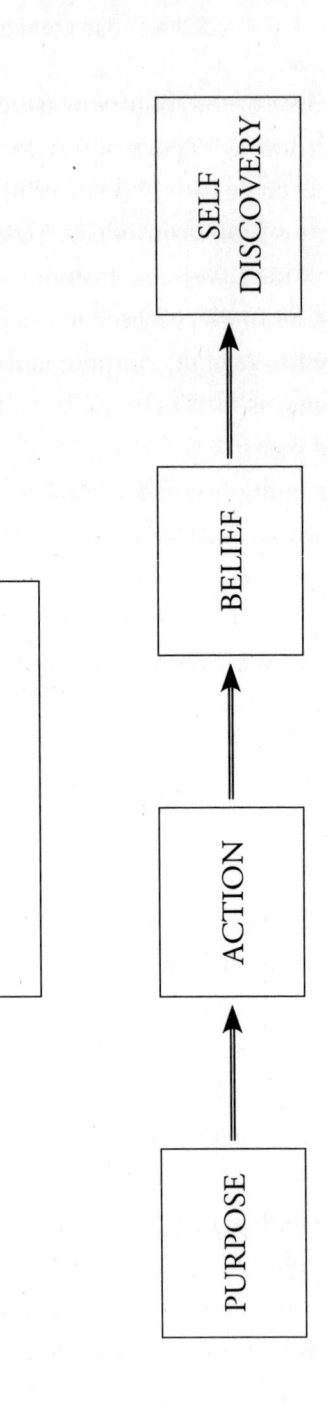

help you achieve your goals and provides a greater sense of freedom and control over your life because it brings structure and time management. This improvement zone strengthens all your goals. It is only through this kind of discipline that we are able to script a path to freedom. Life without discipline is freedom without responsibility, which can be both disastrous and dangerous.

Discipline, therefore, empowers you to say yes or no with conviction and gives you the courage to script your own freedom.

Assessing expectations while freedom is scripted— Expectations and accountability

Conversations are very important because they help us understand whether we have met every expectation. When we desire the kind of freedom we are scripting, we need to understand what it is that we expect. Expectations are closely tied to our goals. Once those goals are clearly defined, they should be used as benchmarks to measure progress, and we must seek regular feedback on our performance. This is the central concept of the course 'Setting Expectations & Assessing Them' by Kris Plachy at UC Davis. The course makes it very clear that feedback and coaching play a crucial role in enhancing the skills, which are tools and knowledge necessary to enjoy that happiness that comes with freedom.

Designing Your Own Freedom Logo

With every script, a beautiful logo can also be created to enhance the understanding of freedom, something that is often done in schools. When children are asked to draw a symbol of freedom, they often draw the school flag, national symbols, or birds in the sky. However, rarely does anything encourage them to think outside the box. I once had a student who drew a unique symbol of freedom - a treasure chest opening up, with beautiful papers flying out of it. According to him, this represented the freedom to share knowledge, the freedom of expression, and the freedom of thought.

Why do we often assume that if we have to draw a rising sun, it must rise from behind hillocks? Why can't the sun rise from somewhere else? We often see it depicted as rising from the ocean horizon or a plain field, but I have also enjoyed the beauty of the sun rising between two skyscrapers in a concrete jungle. The sun always rises and gives you that delight and freedom to think, 'Arise! Awake! And stop not till the goal is reached.' Everybody has their perspective of freedom. So, when they draw their logo, it becomes a reflection of their personal version of that freedom.

What freedom means to me?

For me, freedom is not just a personal journey but a communal one. It's rooted in the hope of creating a world where everyone can flourish without fear or oppression—a world we all strive to build together.

Freedom is a profound concept that holds different meanings for different people. To me, freedom represents the ability to live authentically, express oneself without fear, and make choices that align with one's values and aspirations. It's about having the opportunity to pursue happiness and growth while respecting the freedom and rights of others. Being free open my mind and allows me to think critically.

Open-Mindedness and Critical Thinking

Open-mindedness and critical thinking are essential companions to freedom. They allow us to:

1. Embrace diversity: Open-mindedness is the key to understanding and appreciating different perspectives. It fosters a world where freedom is not just a personal right but a shared and inclusive experience for all.
2. Question assumptions: Critical thinking ensures we challenge beliefs and analyze situations thoughtfully, enabling us to make informed decisions rather than blindly following norms or opinions.

With an open mind, we grow. We evolve through learning, and critical thinking equips us to evaluate new ideas critically yet fairly.

The most important feature in a freedom script should be the act of caring.

Caring in Enjoying Freedom

Caring adds a vital ethical dimension to freedom. It's a reminder that true freedom doesn't exist in isolation—it thrives through community and connection. Caring ensures that we respect others' freedoms, foster empathy, and build meaningful relationships.

1. We respect others' freedoms: Our choices shouldn't infringe on others' rights or well-being.

2. We foster empathy: We recognize the struggles of those
    who may not have the same freedoms and work to address
    inequalities.
3. We build meaningful relationships: Sharing our freedom
    with others enriches our lives and creates a sense of belonging.

Joy in Freedom

Freedom is most fulfilling when it's lived with joy. This comes
from:

- Authentic self-expression: Being able to express who we
  truly are.
- Pursuing passions: Engaging in what makes us happy and
  fulfilled.
- Living without fear: Feeling safe and empowered in our
  choices.

When paired with open-mindedness, critical thinking, and
a caring approach, freedom becomes not just a personal
privilege but a collective responsibility that enriches everyone's
experience. The secret to happiness is freedom. It gives us the
power to fly and follow our heart.

What does freedom mean to you?

Activity

Make your own freedom logo.

—◦✕◦—

For every minute spent organizing, an hour is earned.

15

Organize and Orient

Benjamin Franklin once said, 'For every minute spent in organizing, an hour is earned.' This definitely proves that to be successful, one must first be organized. I have attended many grand events and often found them very disappointing, especially when the entire organizing team did not match up to the standards of the guests. However, at some other similar events where guests were expected to stay only briefly, the excellent management and high level of organization encouraged them to stay longer.

Always make your guests and clients feel valued, rather than involving them merely as a matter of routine invitation. Personally, when we are more organized with our daily schedule, our overall performance increases by another ten per cent, which goes a long way in making life more streamlined and successful.

What are the various ways one could learn to be more organized?

1. Declutter

Numerous people take on more work than they could possibly do, leading to exhaustion and burnout.

They are given so much responsibility that no role is properly organized, resulting in disappointing outcomes. This is particularly because of clutter that conflicts with specific goals. It is highly essential to know how to prioritize work.

Clutter it leads to nothing but work being postponed. One must tell oneself, 'If you do not need it, do not use it; if you cannot do it, do not take it on; and if you find it difficult, don't work on it.' This helps to declutter significantly and is the first step towards learning how to organize yourself.

2. Prioritize

Successful leaders know exactly how to prioritize their work. Ask yourself: what is your priority in life? Many leaders understand this already, but ultimately, whatever makes you happy must be your priority—the thing you put first.

You must rank your tasks in order of importance, and as you do, you'll realize that what ranks number one is what you are passionate about.

When responsibility and tasks are well established, the rest will fall into place. Prioritizing helps you to organize your work and focus your attention effectively. All powerful leaders have the courage to say 'no' to things they don't like, and they say 'yes' to what aligns with their passion.

The best way to organize one's work is by knowing how to prioritize. Tasks must be addressed according to urgency and importance.

Learning how to prioritise work is an art. Below is my method of prioritising:

1. There are some tasks that need to be put on Priority List One and they need to be done urgently. This generally happens when a sudden task comes your way, like a business deal that needs to be closed or a disaster management issue.
2. The next kind of task, second on the priority list, deals with tasks that can be postponed. However, they need to be a marked for a specific deadline in the near or distant future. Your time can be spent on strategizing and planning before carrying out tasks to their completion.
3. The next kind of task implies that it can be assigned to others, such as scheduling appointments, or drafting documents. These tasks are called delegated tasks.
4. A leader can also assign tasks without a strict deadline. These tasks can be handled by their subordinates at their own pace.

I spend about 15 minutes every morning, while sipping my coffee, making a list of every task in order of priority—from the most important to the least important—and noting the time limits for each one. Once the priorities are set, you are aware of what to do next, and that is called planning.

3. Plan

Planning requires a process that is established on three parameters that need equal attention. For a plan to work seamlessly, there has to be a blueprint that helps ensure smooth execution, prevents obstacles, fills gaps, and avoids loopholes and delays.

I have developed an approach to guide one while planning. I call it the 3-Ts: Time, Task, Team.

The first step is to plan on time. Scheduling is very important.

I once knew a leader who spoke of great plans but never set any deadlines. This led the team to think that they could complete tasks at their own pace, based on their individual ability and skill. All good managers and leaders must set and stick to deadlines so that everyone knows the value of time and the importance of completing a given task. For the leader, this also makes it easier and more relevant to assess the team members, the task at hand, and time required to work effectively.

Similarly, when a task is assigned to an individual, it is done after careful evaluation and identification based on their experience. Here, setting a deadline helps to close any potential loopholes by allowing flexibility in different roles and ensuring efficient time management. We have seen time and time again how effective time management helps expedite the completion of tasks.

An example of this can be seen in how a bus tire cannot be changed if the driver and the guard- who together form a team- are not properly appointed. This illustrates why building the right team is so important. The members who make up a team should always include the leader. This is why good organizations always leave it to the leader to form their own team. I firmly believe that leaders create new leaders and gradually, they those leaders to create their own teams to fulfil their requirements. This gives the leader a way to make changes and train everyone.

A good set of rules for an organization should be task—based and focused on deadlines. First and foremost, the task should not feel like a burden. To get rid of this fear, every task should be broken down into smaller, manageable subtasks, with a realistic time frame assigned to each one.

Ensure that all tasks and subtasks are clearly defined at least a day before deadlines are set. It's also important to understand the dependencies between tasks when setting these deadlines. I always recommend including buffer time to help address gaps and make necessary adjustments.

We've emphasized the importance of setting dates to communicate deadlines effectively. This is where time management techniques come into play. Time can be managed using tools such as Google Calendar or scheduling weekly follow-up meetings.

What is a work schedule or a work plan?

A project work schedule requires a specific timeline and work plan that determines start dates, milestones, due dates, activities, and objectives. This helps managers distribute work among the team members and make them understand their responsibilities and work hours, which can increase productivity. As a teacher, I remember when we had to set up a Youth Parliament. We all worked together and achieved excellent productivity by ensuring that the schedule was followed at every step. This approach not only boosted productivity but also increased efficiency and motivation.

Workforce: Identifying the right team members is a key aspect for human resource management. Setting clear work criteria is very necessary for strategic workforce planning, especially when preparing for complex projects like a space journey. The very first step is to find the right kind of team members through rigorous human resource planning. This ensures that the appropriate projects with the necessary skills are hired to meet the project's goals.

Workforce planning involves identifying skills and experience, operational workforce, succession planning, creating new positions, strategizing the workforce, and ultimately a good action plan.

I noticed that my boss never looked stressed, and often wondered how he managed to complete all his work without showing any signs of stress. Some said the boss was simply made that way. While some applauded him for his effective planning, others said he was too clever and knew how to delegate, or even bully people, to get his way. Upon a careful analysis, I could say that his organization skills were just that good, and he made the rules clear to everyone. He realized the importance of providing feedback but without demotivating the workforce. He knew the core members of his team and treated them according to their responsibilities and abilities. This demonstrates the wisdom of identifying the right team members, following up with the team up, and giving feedback without demotivating others.

Many companies of international repute have succeeded because of a strong organizational structure. It may be because of a functional, transitional structure based on expertise, focusing on innovation and quality control. It also could be because of a 'tribe model' structure, which encourages cross-functional teams with high autonomy, promoting rapid innovation and adaptation. Smaller companies follow an amoeba-like structure, especially with small and self-managed units. It is important to take accountability from the very beginning itself.

The above insights are valuable for students, both on a personal level and from a managerial perspective.

Orientation means studying oneself and the workplace before plunging into systematic work. If one learns how to be oriented, any path to learning becomes smoother and less challenging.

There are two types of orientation:

1. Personal orientation
2. Organizational orientation

Personal Orientation

Before getting into organizational orientation, every individual who forms an organization must learn how to identify with themselves. How does this happen?

First, learn to address and identify your own skills. It is very important that we understand our strengths and, according to those strengths, work on a model that would suit us best and make us happy. Many people pursue engineering when they are actually better suited for the life sciences. This is a common issue in developing countries, where people are often carried away by the norms of the society. However, it is perfectly acceptable to work based on one's strengths. One must always think of their own aspirations and desires, and then prioritize accordingly, rather than going along with what seems attractive. I always tell people to put themselves first. It may seem selfish, but only when you are well-trained and are confident can you serve others and guide them. Self-orientation must come before organizational orientation.

The mind also needs to be trained to face challenges and eventualities. That is why it is said: 'Be prepared and train your mind before being taken unawares by situations you have never before experienced.'

Organizational Orientation

Once personal orientation is complete, organizational orientation makes the part to leadership even smoother. There are various kinds of organizational orientation—it can de departmental, or rule-specific. This can also be called the induction programme. Every good organization spends time learning about its employees and employers through a good orientation and induction programme. Students in colleges and schools are also given an orientation before choosing their subjects.

All success stories in companies stem from one important fact: good planning and implementation, which bring clarity and schedule time to complete tasks.

A good orientation programme in any workplace encourages communication and provides good feedback. This helps the organization, and eventually improves its structure. Changes are inevitable in today's dynamic world. If one does not embrace change, then one cannot progress within the organization. A good leader, therefore, treats orientation as a continuous process for strengthening the organization. Learning from and participating in an orientation program not only makes individuals smarter but also more efficient.

Good Practices Adopted by Leaders

- Be prepared in advance with the key points for the orientation, and know exactly which topics need to be covered. Reassurance helps everybody feel very organized and confident, which build trust in the organization, its leadership, and among team members.
- Foster good organizational culture by ensuring that every person—right from those in leadership roles to to those at the lowest rank—is interacting well, maintaining consistent, and is clear about the policies. There should be an atmosphere that encourages open dialogue, because when once the conversation begins, a lot of new ideas are brought up.
- Never make anyone feel intimidated or small.
- A good icebreaker session and a tour of the workplace helps new employees feel at home, leading to faster onboarding. A good organization depends on a good orientation program, and vice versa. Building good relationships always supports effective organization and planning. A prime example of meticulous planning leading to success is the Chandrayaan-3 mission by Indian Space Research Organization. Scientists meticulously planned every aspect of the lunar landing, including potential contingencies,

resulting in a flawless touchdown on the moon despite the challenging terrain. This showcases the power of detailed preparation in complex endeavours like space exploration.

- Perfection is the art of a meticulous mind, and even a slight inclination toward it means the job is already half done. All great battles were won because of meticulous planning of generals. Many options are considered while planning, and the best process is selected, eventually leading to success. Being meticulous leads to a better and organized life.

Empower yourself by reading more.

16

Read to Grow

Reading is not just a means of acquiring knowledge; it's a journey filled with joy and growth. The more you read, the more you know, and the more you know, the more you grow. Knowledge becomes your guiding star, and you're never too old to know that, or set another goal, or dream a new dream.

Reading clubs have recently become very popular, alongside libraries—the conglomeration hub for bookworms.

Open a book, and it opens your mind. Books are more than just a string of words compiled together; they offer new levels of understanding, become your lifelong companions, and and inspired your imagination with dreams. Imagine a day without your reading glasses, unable to read even a page. The situation would feel so catastrophic and make you feel miserable. But the moment you find your glasses, it would feel as though the world came alive again, filled with happiness and fresh ideas the moment you begin reading.

There are different types of reading skills, each with its own unique purpose and benefits. From avid readers who devour every word, to beginners who are just starting their reading journey, to children and adults who read for different reasons—the world of reading is diverse and fascinating.

The first kind of reading is called skimming—this involves quickly flipping through the pages of a book and reading the text without paying close attention to each word. It is done often when one is waiting for a short duration, such as at the dentist's office or a bus station.

The second is called scanning. In this method, the reader browses through the text with the intention of capturing only the most important information. It works like a scanner, and only a few are adept at this kind of reading.

Extensive reading is done only for pleasure. Sometimes, a reader can go through a number of pages without even feeling tired. This kind of reading also helps develop good writing skills.

The fourth type of reading is known as intensive reading, and calls for greater concentration. It is exhaustive and is generally done when preparing for a presentation or conducting research. This is also known as close reading.

With the rise of technology, a new medium of reading has emerged—e-reading. Devices like the Amazon Kindle have gained massive popularity among the youth, who find them a more convenient method of reading. Today, one can also read the news online.

A digital reader can keep me informed about the world while fitting in my pocket, making reading more accessible and maintaining your habit of reading even while travelling. Books, after all, always bring a sense of happiness and pleasure.

Reading

A famous song from the film *Sound of Music* goes, 'When you, read you begin with A-B-C. When you sing, you begin with do-re-mi'. It is true that nothing can begin unless we start from scratch, with the basics.

What would be the ABCs of good reading?

Reading is an intellectual adventure. It sharpens your understanding and deepens your love for the written word. Good reading allows one to learn from the masters, and exposes you to a variety of perspectives. It slowly becomes a dynamic yet integral part of one's life.

If it happens to be an alphabet book with pictures, young readers try to figure out the spelling of various words that correspond to the pictures, and gradually learn to read them. I have seen many children develop an interest in reading after seeing pictures related to the stories. Similarly, when it comes to foreign languages, I have always been interested in decoding and deciphering the new words with the help of images and pictures. In fact, pictographs, reading symbols, and hieroglyphics used in the ancient civilizations encouraged researching and reading.

Developing Good Reading Habits

Read aloud and motivate everybody around you to read, especially young learners. It is essential that, from the elementary stage of schooling, reading aloud and discussions help encourage young learners to read books. In the past, reading aloud was often associated with memorization and rote learning, but it actually helps in transferring knowledge from one person to another. The practice of chanting mantras in the older times, followed by the discussion and deciphering the meaning, was one way of making people learn the mantras. Thus, reading aloud not only becomes meaningful or insightful for you, but also motivates you to read extensively.

It is a good idea to create a dedicated reading space, not only in schools but also at home. A small shelf full of books must be an integral part of everyone's home decor, and one should make it a point to discuss the books that have been displayed. Nowadays, coffee shops have started creating spaces that encourage patrons to read as they enjoy their coffees. It is always a pleasure watching an old man sipping coffee and reading the morning newspaper. Today, many cafés promote longer stats and quiet reading time. When such reading spaces are created, more people are drawn to reading, which in turn promotes knowledge sharing and intellectual engagement.

We are fortunate to live in a time when every part of the world boasts beautiful libraries of national and international significance. A visit to the library should be considered just as important as a visit to any famous tourist spot.

The best gift I ever wish to receive, not only in my childhood but even now, is a book. It could be any kind of book that imparts knowledge and also helps me deal with situations. One time, I came across the wonderful bakery in San Francisco, where a lot of books—old and new—were kept outside with a black card on the top that read: 'Pick One, Leave One', which I found beautiful. The concept allowed people to take a book to read and replace it later with another. This ensures that reading happens continuously, and allows people to read while spending very little on books.

I always make it a habit to re-read books. I remember reading the same book during three stages of my life—as a middle school student, as a postgraduate student, and later in my sixties. Each time, my perspective evolved with age and maturity. One learns to respond to the content positively and understand the mind of the author. Re-reading the same content opens up your mind. While older content may be less valid or outdated, it is definitely acts as the base for the new content.

Develop a habit of enhancing your curiosity through reading about the inspirational lives of others. This enhances your curiosity wonders of the past and encourages a magical curiosity of what the future holds for all of us, serving as a powerful motivator to keep exploring and investigating.

Curious People Sharpen Their Knowledge Through Reading

One of the good habits of reading is to set aside a specific time for it and stick to that schedule. In today's modern world, technology has taken over, yet reading remains a popular form of print media. I once asked an author whether the print media would be totally replaced by technology. The author replied, 'Don't we still have staircases next to the elevators?'

Reading is not a mandatory habit. It is meant to be a fun activity that can grow into into a beautiful passion and addiction. The more you read, the more you know, and gradually the more you grow.

One is never lonely with a book, so the habit of carrying a book every time you travel makes it your friend, guide, philosopher, and your best travel partner.

We not only read to recite and remember, but also to relive characters and incidents. I remember going to New Zealand and wanting to visit Matamata, the Shire of the Hobbits in *The Lord of the Rings* movies. An image I had formed while reading the book perfectly matched the reality of the village, Hobbiton—a fictional village in *The Hobbit* and *The Lord of The Rings* movie trilogy. I was dumbfounded when I saw Machu Picchu, a beautiful ancient town in Peru, which was once a royal estate. It is generally believed that since it was tucked away high in the Andes, very few people living at the foothills or in the mainland were aware of this majestic site, thus protecting it for a long time and allowing it to remain intact. Visiting Machu Pichu transported me to the world of the Incas of the yesteryears, and I felt that every stone of the citadels was recounting their stories.

The grandeur of the Indian temples and monuments bring to mind their creators and rulers, as seen in books. Reading about them is the only way that can revive a chain of thoughts and imagination. For instance, the beautiful Konark Sun Temple in Orissa highlights a high level of technology, based on physics and science, which can amaze any astronomer or engineer who visits the site. A lot of doubts are clarified that arise while reading, therefore bringing to life the past.

To be a researcher, one has to know how to read intensively and extensively—only them can one teach. Reading ignites a spark in every child to write, even in those who otherwise would have found it very difficult to come up with their own ideas. Today, more and more children have become authors, thanks to their imagination that flourishes through reading. Reading also strengthens language and communication skills. I know many people who began writing beautiful poetry after being inspired by poets and their works. If reading is a skill, then writing is an even greater skill.

Reading is a powerful tool that provides immense access to knowledge capable of changing the world. Writing reinforces all that is being read. It is a powerful tool for self-actualization. Good reading expands one's horizon to think, connect, concentrate, and draw accurate inferences from situations. Great revolutions were inspired, and countries were liberated from autocracy, after people read powerful books on democracy and governance. It's true that being an avid reader creates an empowered leader.

Reading to converse and communicate is another skill that must be developed well, as it strengthens cognitive processes. It exercises and stimulates the brain, while also enhancing critical thinking and analytical skills. Good readers may be good debaters and good conversationalists. Reading dialogue improves conversational skills, which in turn with dramatic expression on stage.

All successful stage artists are strong speakers, known for their dialogue delivery. Reading is a lifelong skill that improves memory, and builds a foundation of knowledge, and adds richness to life. Keep reading and never give it up—for a reader is the only one who can listen to the whispers of the wind, enjoy the chirping of the birds, and see the joy in a blooming flower.

Today, a reader; tomorrow, a leader.

Great writers need to be good readers. Maintaining good speaking skills is essential for effective communication with their peers. Good speechwriters are often good readers and know exactly how to be precise and speak with clarity. Reading is a special skill that enhances personal and intellectual growth, helping one face life's challenges. People are able to face life's challenges. Reading is a good exercise that helps stimulate creativity and supports engaging in creative work.

A book, therefore, helps you enjoy aesthetic experiences and participate in social contexts.

Books to Read to Strengthen Reading Skills

- *Exactly What to Say: The Magic Words for Influence and Impact* by Phil M. Jones
- *Say It Well: How to Talk in Public, in Private, and (Especially) When You're Put on the Spot* by D. Terry Szuplat

Activities for Developing Speaking Skills

- Phonics practice (e.g., P, p sounds) using flashcards and matching letters with sounds
- Reading beautiful poetry aloud
- Aural activities (listening and speaking exercises)
- Telling stories with open endings or a twist
- Discussions of book reviews and summaries

Powerful Readings That Have Transformed Perspectives, Inspired, and Reshaped the World

- *The Republic* – Plato
- *The Alchemist* – Paulo Coelho
- *A Brief History of Time* – Stephen Hawking
- *Long Walk to Freedom* – Nelson Mandela
- *To Kill a Mockingbird* – Harper Lee
- *The Bhagavad Gita* – Translated by Eknath Easwaran

About the Author

Kalyani Patnaik is an acclaimed educator and dynamic school leader who has received many awards to her credit as best principal and woman of substance. She was honoured with the Lifetime Achievement Award for Educational Excellence by the Indo-European Excellence Award. She has spearheaded several initiatives, her favourites being the Creative Writing and Reading Club, TEDx, and the HFS MUN, held exclusively and with a different class every year.

An advocate of cultural integration and heritage, she recently initiated a global culture club named Virasat, aimed at nurturing cross-cultural appreciation among students. Having travelled extensively across India and the world, Kalyani Patnaik brings global perspectives and best practices into her educational philosophy, enriching her institution and the communities she serves.

Scan QR code to access the
Penguin Random House India website